Sacred
is
the
Call

Sacred is the Call

Formation and Transformation in Spiritual Direction Programs

SUZANNE M. BUCKLEY,
Editor

A Crossroad Book
The Crossroad Publishing Company
New York

The Crossroad Publishing Company
16 Penn Plaza – 481 Eighth Avenue, Suite 1550
New York, NY 10001

Printed in the United States of America

The text of this book is set in 11/15 Esta.
The display face is Worstveld Sting.

Library of Congress Cataloging-in-Publication Data

Sacred is the call : formation and transformation in spiritual direction
programs / Suzanne M. Buckley, editor.
    p. cm.
  Includes bibliographical references.
  ISBN 0-8245-2338-5 (alk. paper)
  1. Spiritual direction. I. Buckley, Suzanne M.
BX2350.7.S33 2005
253.5'3 – dc22

                                               2005021632

1 2 3 4 5 6 7 8 9 10   10 09 08 07 06 05

*To the many Sisters of Mercy who have responded
to a call to the ministry of spiritual direction,
but especially to my teachers at Mercy Center, Burlingame:
Mary Ann Scofield, Marguerite Buchanan, and Suzanne Toolan.*

Sacred is the Call
Awesome indeed the entrustment
Tending the Holy
Tending the Holy

May Christ live in your hearts, through faith may he be with you
That rooted and built in love
You may proclaim his goodness.

For this I pray to God
That you be given power in Christ's Spirit that you may grow —
— grow in inner strength.

Behold then in your prayer —
Approach our God in trust —
For you are God's work, you are God's work of art

So stand your ground in truth —
Hold fast the shield of faith —
Proclaim the gospel of peace in eager, honest deed.

Sacred is the Call
Awesome indeed the entrustment
Tending the Holy
Tending the Holy

SUZANNE TOOLAN, RSM

Contents

GROUNDED IN THE REAL

EVOLUTION /
MOVING WITH THE SPIRIT

Foreword

In the thirty-plus years since I traded in my psychotherapy hat to become a spiritual director and trainer of spiritual directors there has been an explosion of interest in spirituality and spiritual direction. From small beginnings in a few places we now see centers for spirituality and spiritual direction all over the world. Training programs for spiritual directors have proliferated. Spiritual Directors International has grown from a small seed planted in a conference in the early 1990s at Mercy Center in Burlingame, California, to the present organization whose numbers exceed fifty-four hundred and whose members circle the globe.

This book is one witness to this explosion. It is primarily the outgrowth of the training program for spiritual directors at Mercy Center, Burlingame, but includes training personnel from other centers. In it readers will find most of the salient questions facing the profession of spiritual direction and training programs. These questions are faced honestly and forthrightly and with an irenic spirit. In addition, those who conduct training programs will be able to compare what they are doing with these practitioners because most of the articles discuss and demonstrate how things are done in one center.

This will be a very helpful book, another sign that the profession is moving into full adulthood. I hope the book has many readers.

WILLIAM A. BARRY, SJ

Introduction

As the ministry of spiritual direction has expanded in recent years, formation programs to support those called to this vocation have grown rapidly. Because the call to spiritual direction is indeed sacred, this book explores formation programs as journeys of faith. The authors, all spiritual directors with years of experience in designing respected programs, share their wisdom concerning this journey through reflection, commentary, and guidance. Their essays include the core assumptions of formation programs, methods of presentation, the basic topics presented, and questions to consider for "opening up" those topics.

Sacred Is the Call presents an overview of essential program topics. Exploring these topics supports the formation process by enabling participants to move to a deeper level, resulting in a profound experience of personal maturity, freedom, and transformation. This, the authors and I believe, is the space in which we all must reside if we are truly to "tend the Holy."

The material presented here offers a model for formation programs to use in planning their courses; it also supports those already engaged in this work. The text is designed to be a practical help to program staff as well as to be used as class material. With that in mind, the chapters are divided into four sections. Each section contains topics that build upon each other to create a flow of information, exploration, and experience. Each chapter supports a particular theme through theory, examples, research, or practical teaching approaches. Each chapter is followed by questions for further discussion to use with groups and staff, and additional resources for further study.

The first section, Awareness of the Presence, reflects the assumption that authentic formation programs are always grounded in the human experience of God. Foundational to the study of spiritual direction, the essays in this section provide the starting point for an organic evolution of awareness, learning, and application of that assumption. James Neafsey reminds us that our work as human beings is to wake up to the mystery of God's presence and action in all human experience. He considers how this holy work leads to programs that support the formation of spiritual directors who can ground these abstract truths in their lives and help others to do the same.

Understanding the theory and practice of spiritual direction, Rose Mary Dougherty suggests, leads us to acknowledge spiritual direction as an act of prayer. Her profoundly simple essay provides an intentional framework for our own experience of spiritual direction. Maria Tattu Bowen presents us with a beautiful reflection on the nature of contemplation and introduces the notion that spiritual direction is contemplative listening. Joseph D. Driskill examines the essential role of prayer in spiritual direction, both in the lives of director and directee, as well as in the direction session itself. Mary Ann Scofield looks at the importance of the process of discernment in the ministry of spiritual direction and provides concrete examples of listening to and responding to the experience of God in the life of a directee. She concludes the section with an essay introducing the notion of resistance and the importance of recognizing the blocks and fears that stand in the way of deeper awareness which allows us to be more present to oneself, others, and the Holy One.

In the second section, Open to the Mystery, we investigate topics that support spiritual directors as they listen to the varieties of human experience. These subjects are staples of authentic formation programs, and provide direction in exploring human spiritual and psychological development. James Neafsey guides us to an understanding of the stages of prayer life as expressed in the writings of Teresa of Ávila and John of the Cross, still vibrant and helpful to a director today. Patricia Coughlin puts forward some important ideas about the components best covered in programs that carefully present the fluid boundaries between psychological and spiritual aspects of the human journey. James M. Bowler offers a critical lens for viewing the stages of adult spiritual development. Lucy Abbott Tucker invites us to deep listening through the wisdom of the body, and Sandra Lommasson focuses on the important role of sexuality in the process of direction. Donald Bisson concludes the section with a framework for consideration of gender issues in the formation of directors.

The third section, Grounded in the Real, describes several elements of formation programs that provide challenges for staff and participants alike. Interns in spiritual direction programs are not only recipients of knowledge; they must apply their learning and receive additional instruction through ongoing supervision. Program participants are also guided in the accepted ethical norms for the ministry. James M. Keegan provides a realistic reflection on the psychological dynamics existing in the supervision practicum. Sandra Lommasson enlightens us on the topic of dual relationships; when interns begin to work with directees in communities of faith, the complexity of boundary issues surface. Bill Creed's essay calls those in the ministry to move from compassionate listening to compassionate justice; he outlines the areas of moral responsibility involved in the spiritual direction conversation.

The final section, Evolution: Moving with the Spirit, provides an invitation to incorporate some new topics in formation programs as a response to the prophetic nature of the ministry of spiritual direction. The authors cover both the broader movement of the Holy Spirit as we pay attention to where this ministry is leading us, and the personal challenge to all those involved in formation programs as the parameters of spiritual direction expand globally, across faith traditions, to new generations and to what we call "the margin."

Donald Bisson urges formation programs to provide a place for discernment of call to those on the margins. He provides some guidelines to help staff and programs move their participants from self-care to care of the world soul. Sandra Lommasson challenges programs to "widen the tent" by encompassing the ways in which the

Spirit crosses traditional faith boundaries without sacrificing deep rootedness in a particular tradition. Bill Creed advocates for the new generation of spiritual directors and reveals the gifts and concerns of the young adults who will follow us in this ministry. Janice Farrell provides a graced and practical guide for planning and developing a variety of models of group spiritual direction, which she sees as an answer to a deep need and hunger for hope, joy, and love whose source is in God.

The last word belongs to Mary Ann Scofield, who has been so instrumental in moving the discussion of this ministry to the global arena. Mary Ann reminds us of the prophetic nature of spiritual direction and the challenge of seeing the world the way God sees it. As our spiritual lives develop through formation and work as directors, God's love is poured into our hearts until we find that others' joys and sorrows literally become our own. She suggests that our deeper relationship with God moves us, willingly or not, into standing with the poor and working against the unjust structures of our world.

We believe that the true impact of a spiritual direction formation program is not simply the real personal growth that can take place in the participants. As those in spiritual direction programs awaken to the mystery of God's presence and action in all human experience, they reach out to help others recognize the work of the Sacred in their lives. The experience of personal transformation moves program participants to use their gifts at the compassionate service of their families, churches, and communities. They provide direction to others, start prayer groups, lead retreats, and take leadership roles in their faith communities. Others teach Centering Prayer to the incarcerated, serve the destitute in nations ranging from Australia to Zambia, work with elderly, ill, and marginalized people of all ages and types, and develop programs to serve Hispanics and the rural poor. The Spirit has called them. By their fruits you shall know them.

SUZANNE M. BUCKLEY

AWARENESS OF
THE PRESENCE

The Human Experience of God

Where do we find God? As humans and seekers of the Holy, what is our primary life (or spiritual) task? What does spiritual direction have to do with our experience of God? These three questions, and their answers, ground formation programs for spiritual directors. They provide the core theological understanding and spiritual assumptions that permeate every aspect of formation and spiritual direction. I'd like to share with you the responses to these questions that have guided my work.

First, where do we find God?

The Mystery of God is fully present and active in all human experience.

We live and move and have our being in the presence of Divine Mystery whether we are explicitly aware of the presence and transforming power of that Mystery or not.

Second, as humans and seekers of the Holy, what is our primary life (or spiritual) task?

Our human vocation is to wake up to the mystery of God's presence and action in all human experience.

We are called to awaken from the sleep of habitual patterns of thinking, feeling, and acting that obscure our consciousness of God and consent to God's transforming action in the full spectrum of our human experience.

And, finally, what does spiritual direction have to do with our experience of God?

The purpose of spiritual direction is to help people become aware of the mystery of God's presence and action in human experience, and to assist them in making a fuller and freer response to it.

When these assumptions are presented in formation programs, the focus is not on rigorous philosophical and theological exploration of the meaning of "God" and "human experience." Though such exploration is important and valid in other contexts, the primary concern in formation is grounding these abstract truths in personal experience or, to put it another way, to allow intellectual information to catalyze spiritual transformation.

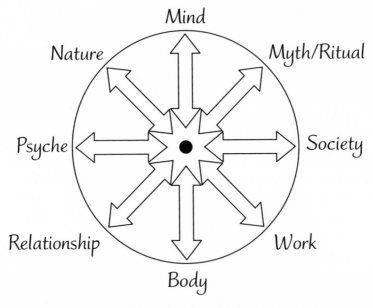

The Circle of Life

The Circle of Life is a teaching tool that has proved useful in clarifying these foundational assumptions and grounding them in the lives of program participants. Around the periphery of the circle are eight realms — mind and body, psyche and society, work and relationship, nature and myth/ritual — that express something of the scope and variety of human experience. Though differentiated from one another for the purpose of conceptual clarity, in reality these eight realms are interwoven in rich and complex ways. The star at the center symbolizes the core of the human spirit, our distinctive capacity to relate to the things of life and to be aware or unaware, willing or unwilling, responsive or unresponsive to them. The double arrows between the center and periphery suggest a dynamic relationship between our spiritual core and the eight realms that comprise ordinary human experience. We are shaped by our experiences in these realms, but we also shape them through the quality of our awareness and the choices we make.

So where is God in all this? All the major wisdom traditions of the world recognize a hunger in the human spirit that goes beyond relationship to the tangible realms of life. We long for Something or Someone More, a relationship to the unfathomable Mystery that flows through all of life but transcends what can be seen or felt with the senses or known in concepts and images. Mystics and theologians have called this Mystery by many names — Ground of Being, Eternal Thou, Infinite Horizon, the All, Brahman, Tao, God. Each tradition names the Mystery in its own way, but all acknowledge that its fullness exceeds our human ability to comprehend or control.

The double arrows, then, can carry a second level of meaning. They represent not just the activity of the human spirit, but also the presence and action of God's Spirit in all eight realms of human experience. These realms are focal points where a dynamic dialogue takes place between the Spirit of God and the human spirit, between the Divine Mystery and our personal awareness of and response to that Mystery.

There are two radically different ways in which we can relate to God in our human experience. In the first mode, we are blind and closed to the Mystery, caught in calculative and controlling relationships to people and things, intent on imposing our own agendas and confirming our own egos. We relate to the people and things of life as "here for me" rather than as having unique identities in their own right. In this mode we remain fixated on the surface of life, unaware and unresponsive to the subtle currents of Spirit that flow in the depths of human experience.

In the second mode, we are aware of and open to Mystery, rooted in contemplative awareness, free to let other people and things be who and what they are in their uniqueness and otherness. We are "here for God" rather than for the preservation and enhancement of our own ego. We have the capacity to discern spiritual meanings and values and have an intuitive awareness of the presence of God dwelling and acting at the depths of human experience.

Moving from the first to the second mode involves a lifelong process of awakening and spiritual conversion in all dimensions of life. Spiritual awakening can happen in many ways. Sometimes awareness of the Mystery breaks through in peak experiences of personal fulfillment, overwhelming beauty, profound gratitude, deep love and joy, or some other experience that reveals the Glory hidden beneath the surface. At other times the Mystery manifests through experiences of failure, loss, disillusionment, conflict, darkness, and pain. As our normal beliefs and support systems are stripped away or found empty and inadequate in the face of these harsh realities, we discover a sustaining Divine Ground that remained unnoticed while all was functioning well at the surface. We can also awaken in less dramatic ways. We gradually grow into a steady, quiet awareness of Mystery as always — and already — there in the background of ordinary experience. The presence of God shines forth in simple things — sunlight pouring through a window, the steady faithfulness of a spouse, the kindness of strangers, and the daily routine of prayer.

The role of the director is to accompany others on this journey of spiritual awakening. Directors help others to become aware of God's presence and invitations to deeper intimacy in the human experiences of their lives. The director assists others to articulate these experiences, savor them slowly, and integrate them over time. The primary resource directors bring to such a task is their own spiritual sensitivity to the Divine Mystery at the heart of life. If they have listened deeply for God in their own experience, they will be better equipped to hear God in the lives of others.

Meditation on the Circle of Life

After the basic concepts outlined above have been presented and clarified through examples, participants are invited to apply them to their own experience through a guided meditation based on the Circle of Life. In the meditation, they are asked to focus attention on their lives at this present moment, to wait and listen for feelings, sensations, images, or words that capture the quality of their human experience as a whole. Then time is allowed for exploring each of the eight realms of the Circle of Life in greater detail.

For example, the leader of the meditation might say, "Sense how it is with your body at this time ... What is your overall feeling about your body? ... What is the state of your health? ... Your experience of pleasure and pain? ... Your sense of the joys and limits of bodily life at this moment of your life? ... What invitations to fuller awareness and response are you experiencing in the realm of the body? ... How do you experience the Mystery of God there?"

After similar meditations on the remaining seven realms are presented, participants are invited to reflect in silence and record in their journals what came up for them, noting especially those realms where they were most and least aware of God's presence and activity. Then they are given time to share their reflections in dyads and in the full group.

This exercise helps ground in specific personal experiences the general statement that God is present and active in all human experience. Most participants notice that they are more aware of the Mystery of God in some realms than in others. For example, an individual may report being vividly aware of God in the realms of psyche and relationship, while God's presence in the realms of work and society seems vague and less compelling. Another may speak about a keen sense of God's activity in movements for social justice in the realm of society, but have little sense of how God is acting in the psyche, the inner world of dreams, imagination, memory, and feeling. Noticing such patterns helps participants identify assumptions and mental filters that blind them to God's presence in significant realms of human experience. This kind of reflection on the ways in which personal bias, cultural conditioning, and unconscious assumptions can block awareness of the experience of God is at the core of the transformational learning involved in the formation of directors. At a later stage of formation, this type of exploration of the mental filters that affect our awareness and response to another's experience of God will be a principal focus of individual supervision.

A Curriculum for Spiritual Formation

The three foundational questions and responses to them, the Circle of Life, and the meditation exercise described above can be presented as topics for a single class early in a formation program. These topics can also be developed into a curriculum for the entire first year of a program focused primarily on the personal spiritual formation of participants.[1] Following an opening weekend retreat, an overview of the Circle of Life and reflections on the contemplative attitude toward experience are presented in the first regular monthly class. Each of the remaining monthly sessions of the first year focus on one or two of the eight realms in greater depth. For example, the realm of myth/ritual is explored on a day devoted to Praying with Sacred Story and Ritual. Society is the focus in a class called Listening for God in the World. A retreat weekend explores the themes of Listening for God in the Body and Nature. The entire year becomes an extended meditation on the Circle of Life, a long, loving look at the Mystery of God present and active in lived human experience.

Between class meetings, participants are asked to relate the monthly theme to their life experience in a short reflection paper. These papers challenge participants to become aware of the presence of God in one particular realm of the Circle of Life and to articulate their experience in writing. A second monthly paper invites participants to reflect concretely on their awareness of and response to God in all eight realms of the Circle of Life. Staff mentors respond to both papers each month with written feedback that further personalizes the learning process.

Holistic Teaching and Learning

The teaching methods employed in this program are also grounded in the understanding that the Mystery of God is present and active in all human experience. Assigned readings and didactic presentations that engage the mind are balanced with movement and dance that engage the body. Attention to individual memory, symbolic expression, and personal story (the realm of psyche) is balanced with attention to group spirit and community dialogue (the realm of society). The importance of personal relationship in the learning process is fostered by regular participation in dyads, triads, and small mentor groups. The realm of myth/ritual is honored by weaving sacred story, poetry, song, and simple rituals into the day at several points. The schedule attempts to honor the need for focused work as well as relaxation and play in the learning process. Though the urban neighborhood in which the class meets is not conducive to spending much time in nature, weekend retreats in a beautiful setting are planned twice during the year. These holistic modes of learning are intended to cultivate an awareness of the presence and transformative power of God in various types of experience.

The feedback regarding the content and methods of this formation year has been quite positive. Participants speak of increased sensitivity to the presence of God in a wide range of human experience. By the end of the year, they are able to articulate in concrete terms their particular strengths and areas of weakness regarding awareness and response to God in the eight realms of life. The foundational assumptions concerning God's presence in all human experience and the human vocation to wake up and respond to that presence are made specific and personal over the course of the year through the integration of class content, reflection papers, holistic teaching methods, individual spiritual direction, and the sharing of life experiences and personal stories in community.

In the first year of the program, relatively little attention is given to the theory and practice of spiritual direction itself. Instead, the primary focus is on personally assimilating the foundational assumptions that underlie spiritual direction through the content and practices described above. Through the intellectual and spiritual disciplines offered in the program, participants develop a deeper awareness of God, a broader understanding of prayer, practical self-knowledge, increased vocabulary to articulate spiritual experience, and a growing capacity to trust and listen contemplatively to other members of the group. The experiences, skills, and insights related to listening for God in human experience that are developed in this initial year provide a solid foundation for further stages in formation that are concerned more immediately with the actual practice of spiritual direction.

For Further Reflection

1. How might you describe your core theological assumptions as you enter spiritual direction formation?

2. In which realms of your life — body, mind, society, relationship, work, nature, psyche, myth/ritual — are you most aware of God's presence?

3. In which realms are you least aware of God's presence?

4. What kind of mental filters, assumptions, beliefs might get in the way of your awareness of God's presence in your life?

Resources

Barry, William A. *With an Everlasting Love: Developing an Intimate Relationship with God.* Mahwah, N.J.: Paulist Press, 1999.

Edwards, Denis. *Human Experience of God.* Mahwah, N.J.: Paulist Press, 1983.

Rohr, Richard. *Everything Belongs: The Gift of Contemplative Prayer.* New York: Crossroad, 2003.

Shea, John. *An Experience Named Spirit.* Chicago: Thomas More Press, 1983.

Experiencing the Mystery of God's Presence
The Theory and Practice of Spiritual Direction

The theory or understanding of spiritual direction is, I believe, a dynamic reality, something that will deepen and change as we experience the mystery of God's presence in our direction sessions. Our practice of spiritual direction must both honor and reflect our understanding of it. Otherwise it loses its vitality, perhaps somewhat as our prayer does when we hold on to old forms that no longer honor and reflect what seems to be going on between God and ourselves.

An Understanding of Spiritual Direction

My understanding of spiritual direction and its practice grows out of thirty years of experience of both giving and receiving spiritual direction and participating in a colleague group. My years of prayer and dialogue with my colleagues in spiritual direction formation work and other spiritual directors have further refined it. I offer what fits for me, and what I and others have espoused over the years. It may not fit for you. I hope, however, that my reflections will encourage you to claim more wholeheartedly what you believe about spiritual direction and to allow that belief to more intentionally inform your practice of it.

As I begin, then, I invite you to take a few minutes to reflect on your experiential understanding of spiritual direction. If you are a spiritual director, you might ask yourself questions like these: "What are the times when I have been with a directee that I have I felt most fully

alive and authentic as a spiritual director? What has characterized
these times? What did they have in common? From these experiences
how would I name/describe the heart of spiritual direction? What is
the core of my calling as a spiritual director?" As a directee you might
ask yourself questions like these: "When I first felt the invitation to
be in spiritual direction, what was I looking for? What am I looking
for now? When are the times in spiritual direction that I feel as if I
have touched the heart of spiritual direction? What went on during
those times that made it real spiritual direction for me? How would I
describe to a friend what spiritual direction is for me?" Let what you
have uncovered in this reflection be the backdrop for your further
reading.

Spiritual Direction as Prayer

Put quite simply, I would describe spiritual direction as an act of
prayer. When I say "an act of prayer," I am referring to those times
when we consciously choose to put ourselves in the way of grace, or
to enter the sacred space of our True Self, or open ourselves to the
Indwelling Mystery of our souls. In speaking of spiritual direction
as an act of prayer, I might also describe it as a time of intentional
availability to God on the part of both the director and the directee for
the sake of the deepening discernment of the directee. This shared
act of prayer is the acknowledgment that the Holy Spirit is, indeed,
the spiritual director and that the time together is about creating an
atmosphere supportive of detached listening and fresh seeing. In this
time of prayer, both director and directee are transformed.

This prayer of spiritual direction begins in directors as a response
to God's invitation and gift of a call to be a spiritual director. In
prayer, they seek out the appropriate means to nurture and perhaps
to prune the expression of the call already taking root. They also
look for a spiritual community of other directors who will support
them in an ongoing way in faithfulness to their call. This community
supports directors in a variety of ways: by praying with them, by
lending their eyes to help them see their blind spots and areas of

unfreedom as a spiritual director, and by celebrating the times of grace-filled awareness.

The Spiritual Direction Relationship

Directors intentionally bring the decision about whether or not to enter into a particular direction relationship to prayer. Here, they may ask themselves questions like these: "Do I sense God inviting us to be together? Is there anything about the directee that pushes me into my agenda for the person, that gets in the way of my prayerfulness? Do I sense in myself a reverence for the Divine in the person?" If they decide to enter the direction relationship, they make a commitment to pray for the directee and they periodically return to the prayer of discernment alone and with the directee about the rightness of continuing in the relationship. Finally, but perhaps most importantly, the directors seek to be a praying presence with directees during the time of their meetings. Together they choose practices that might support their prayerfulness.

Everything that I have said of the prayer of spiritual direction for directors may also be said for directees, beginning with the felt need, the call, to explore spiritual direction and the discerning prayer about who might be right to serve as spiritual director. In this discernment directees might ask questions like these: "Do I sense a freedom to be myself with this person/ to say what seems to be given to me to say? Do I feel supported by the director in my own discerning process, or am I relying on the director to discern for me? Am I able to be in a prayerful place with this director?" Once having entered the relationship, directees make a commitment to pray for directors and to consider prayerfully from time to time the appropriateness of continuing with a particular director. Directees, too, share responsibility for the prayerfulness of the direction time.

Once the initial gatherings for getting acquainted and discerning the rightness of being together in direction are completed, direction sessions usually happen about once a month. This timing is a way of honoring the direction of the Spirit in directees' lives and the responsibility of directees for living a discerning life. In preparation for the meeting directees may pray through their journals and reflect on what they might bring. Directors, too, will pray to be open to what is shown them and may even get a glimpse of what they think the session might be about. However, the real "agenda" for the meeting is God's and usually only becomes apparent as director and directee sit in prayer together. There they open themselves to see freshly what is given them to see in that moment and look at it as seems appropriate in that moment, within the context of prayer.

Recently I was exploring with someone the rightness of being in spiritual direction together. After he shared with me why he was looking for spiritual direction now and I shared something of my understanding of what spiritual direction was about, he began to talk about his life, including the times he had been in therapy. When he finished, he said to me, "Now that you've heard what I'm about, what do you think we will work on if I'm in spiritual direction with you?" He was initially taken aback when I said, "We won't work on anything. That's up to you and God. We'll see what God brings up and how God wants you to be with it. That will be yours to pray about. I can't tell you what to see but I may be able offer some help in ways of seeing, and noticing the places you are choosing not to look."

We decided to begin to meet regularly and to begin our times with some silence together. In each of our three meetings he has begun his sharing with something like, "I thought I might talk about one thing, but this is what came up when I was sitting here." What I have noticed in our conversations is that he seems to be spending more time outside of our meetings praying about the significance of events in his life, noticing the God-connecting threads among them, whereas before he was waiting for our time together to do that. That prayer is becoming part of him, and he brings it to our meetings. His prayerful spirit is grounding for me. I find myself more honoring the mystery of his process and less apt to push to make something happen. My times with him are becoming an explicit reminder of that which I believe implicitly, that is, that God and the person are already together. It is not mine to create the relationship but to witness to its unfolding, and to assist the other's appreciation of it and participation in it as I can. The prayer of spiritual direction creates a space where this can happen.

It is in my experiences of accompanying the dying that I have been brought most profoundly and consistently into the prayer of spiritual direction. In these experiences, I rarely think about how I can help the person, what I can do for them. Rather, I am usually given to realize that there is deep mysterious process going on that is not mine to see. I can only stand in reverent awe and service of it. I may bring to the dying person my experience of being with them in the past, or things that I have read or learned from being with others that may be of assistance. But this is a new moment, and I see clearly that despite all I think I know, I don't know what is here, now, in this moment. So I pause at the sacred threshold of this moment in the prayer of not-knowing presence. Here I wait to be shown my place of entry, and what is mine to do or leave undone.

And so it is with spiritual direction. I may have been meeting with someone for fifteen years; I may have acquired much knowledge and many skills that have been useful in spiritual direction at other times. But this is a new moment. I pause at the sacred threshold of this moment, suspending all my knowing and my skills, and wait to be shown my place of entry. I bow in reverent awe before the Mystery. I am drawn into the prayer of spiritual direction and am transformed.

For Further Reflection

1. What image do you hold of spiritual direction? Describe.

2. How might you describe spiritual direction to someone who knows nothing about it?

3. When you first felt the invitation to be in spiritual direction, what were you looking for? What are you looking for now?

4. What moves in you as you consider spiritual direction as an act of prayer? How might you name what you are feeling?

🌼 Resources

Bakke, Jeannette. *Holy Invitations: Exploring Spiritual Direction*. Grand Rapids, Mich.: Baker Book House, 2000.

Dougherty, Rose Mary. *Group Spiritual Direction: Community for Discernment*. Mahwah, N.J.: Paulist Press, 1995.

Edwards, Tilden. *Spiritual Director/Spiritual Companion: Guide to Tending the Soul*. Mahwah, N.J.: Paulist Press, 2001.

Kelly, Thomas. *A Testament of Devotion*. San Francisco: HarperSanFrancisco, 1996.

Singh, Kathleen Dowling. *The Grace in Dying: How We Are Transformed Spiritually as We Die*. San Francisco: HarperSanFrancisco, 1998.

Hearing with the Heart
Contemplative Listening in the Spiritual Direction Session

"Listen," I say. I hold the Tibetan bowl aloft and strike it with a wooden stick. "What do you hear?"

"Music," one student answers.

"A chord," says another.

"Vibrations," a third observes.

"You know what I hear?" I ask. "I hear Tibetan monks in red robes with saffron wraps walking along a path to their temple." Many hands raise simultaneously.

"I hear a warm breeze."

"I hear a mandala."

"I hear the Dalai Lama."

Then I say, "When I listen to myself and the bowl at the same time, I hear my heart grow peaceful." Again, multiple hands wave.

"I hear my sadness that the Tibetan monks are in exile."

"I hear my excitement when I went on my first Buddhist retreat."

"I hear myself settling down."

What Is Contemplative Listening?

In these opening moments of our[2] contemplative listening course, the first course students take in the spiritual direction program in which I teach, students listen not only with their ears but also with their hearts, their minds, and the rest of their bodies.

33

To contemplate is to consider something or someone fully, deeply — so fully, so deeply, in fact, that we encounter the truth of them, that we perceive a whiff of the sacred emanating from them. Indeed, we fall with them into the love of God. How appropriate, then, that the word "contemplate" has at its root the word "temple," that place where we meet the sacred.

Like contemplation, listening involves paying attention, an activity Simone Weil equates with prayer.[3] One definition of listening particularly appropriate for use with directors in training comes from the International Listening Association: "[Listening is] the process of receiving, constructing meaning from, and responding to spoken and/or nonverbal messages."[4]

Receiving. Constructing meaning. Responding. The sum of these activities done with full attention in the context of the God within whom we live, and move, and have our being is one way to begin thinking about contemplative listening. But who do we listen to? And what do we listen for?

While practicing contemplative listening in the context of spiritual direction, we listen in faith to the directee and to ourselves, confident that in doing so we will also hear God. God's prompting and invitation is what we listen for. It's a tall order, listening at the same time to the directee, to ourselves, and to God, one that proves challenging for most directors, beginning and otherwise. It is not surprising, then, that this course in contemplative listening is one that we instructors call students back to again and again throughout their training period, both during class and in practice groups.

Teaching Contemplative Listening

In our experience, instructing beginning directors in contemplative listening is best accomplished in two phases, each featuring lecture, discussion, and practice. In the first phase, we challenge students to grow in their awareness of themselves and of the myriad of ways in which they can perceive God in their own experience. In the second, we provide detailed instruction about how to perceive God in human experience, and students develop greater awareness of others by participating in small group activities designed to help them listen to directees, even as they attempt to continue to hear themselves and God. By the end of the term, most students have had multiple experiences of contemplative listening, experiences in which they are conscious of hearing and responding to themselves, others, and God.

Now let's look at some examples of course and practice-group content for instructing spiritual directors in contemplative listening.

Phase One / Listening to Self and God in Personal Experience

Phase one highlights dimensions of human experience. Lectures and discussions focus on noticing thoughts, feelings, and sensations. Approximately three hours is spent on each of these dimensions. An additional six hours of course work concentrates on categories that incorporate more than one dimension of experience, such images and metaphors. Class sessions focus on how to listen contemplatively to the dimension of human experience at hand, for example, thoughts, feelings, or sensations, and how to work with it in spiritual direction.

We do this by presenting theological instruction from the work of Karl Rahner and John Calvin to ground students in the idea that God's presence can be perceived human experience. Students tend to learn best in this phase by practicing and debriefing in the large group, which has been designed to help them develop more and more subtle ways of listening to their own experience. For example, before we have presented much information about contemplative listening, we ask students to recall a time when they felt loved and then to write about it, fleshing it out until they remember the thoughts they were having at the time, the sensations they felt in their bodies, and the feelings kindled by the experience.

Once they have finished writing, we ask students to record the sensations, thoughts, and feelings that arise for them now, in the present moment, as they remember their past experience. Then, we debrief the practice as a class. Instead of focusing on the content of their past experience, or even about the thoughts, sensations, and feelings associated with it, we look at what they noticed in the process of remembering it.

Inevitably someone mentions that as she recalled her experience, she began to think similar thoughts, to feel similar sensations and emotions as she did during the original experience. Someone else usually adds that the thoughts, sensations and feelings he had in the present moment seem somehow even richer now, accompanied as they are by the new thoughts, feelings, and sensations stirred by remembering. Eventually a student will name his or her experience of love as an experience of God. Then we pose this question: "If no one had named their experience an experience of God, would it still *be* an experience of God?" Most students readily assert that it would. This begins to free our directors-in-training from feeling as if they are not doing spiritual direction unless the directee speaks explicitly about God.

This practice helps students become more adept at detecting the contours of their own experience and at listening to themselves while in the midst of experiencing. It challenges those who aren't used to thinking of ordinary human experience as experience of God to begin to consider that this could be the case. It also draws out of the students a conscious experience of contemplative listening. They receive their own experience. They respond in the spontaneous experiencing of thoughts, sensations, and feelings similar to those they had in the initial experience. They construct meaning as the initial thoughts, sensations, and feelings are enriched now by new ones, and as they name their experience as an experience of God.

Phase Two / Growing in Awareness of Self, Others, and God

During phase two of contemplative listening class, we explore together particular opportunities for noticing God's presence in human experience, including the moments when freedom, desire, consolation, invitation, and the fruits of the Spirit arise during spiritual direction sessions. In addition, we investigate what can block the ability to notice God's presence (for example, pain, fatigue, abuse, illness, fear, despair, and distorted images of God).

In this phase, students continue growing in self-awareness and awareness of God. Now, however, they must learn to become aware of another person at the same time as they participate in contemplative listening groups each day.[5] In preparation for these practice groups, students write a précis, one to three paragraphs long, describing an experience. This description includes not only the event as it occurred but also the thoughts, feelings, sensations, and desires that accompanied it. Often students wrack their brains for memories of mountaintop experiences. However, we encourage them to select instead some ordinary, though moving experience: a walk on the beach, perhaps, or an encounter with a smiling child; we explain our assumption that God is present at all times and in every area of our lives, so that if we pay prayerful attention to an experience, no matter how ordinary, we can encounter God's transforming presence.

In each practice-group session, one student serves as a focus person and another as group facilitator. The focus person reads his or her précis aloud and responds to input from the group. The facilitator keeps time, marks the beginning and end of each phase of the process, and slows the group down if necessary.

As group members listen to the précis, they attempt pay attention to the words, voice, and body language of the focus person even as they listen to their own responses: the thoughts, feelings, and sensations that arise in them as they listen. After the reading, the facilitator invites the group to sit in silence, at which point group members grapple with what they have heard, sifting it all until they discern which idea, image, metaphor, feeling, or sensation emerges as one most powerfully inviting their attention.

When the facilitator senses that adequate silence has passed, he or she invites group members to respond to the focus person. They begin doing so, often straining at first against limits imposed to train them in the art of responding gently: they must confine their remarks to statements about what they have noticed. In short, students ask no questions, nor do they make comments other than those drawn directly from the précis, the focus person's reading of it, their personal reaction to it, or the responses of the group subsequent to the reading.

The facilitator insures that the rate of the group's responses is slow, allowing adequate time for the focus person to absorb each offering, to gauge what he or she notices inside while doing so, and to respond verbally to it, sometimes adding further information relevant to the original story. For example, a focus person reads a précis about a walk in the woods. At some point, a listener says, "I notice that the woods were dark." The focus person responds, "Yes, they were especially dark that day." A pause, and then she continues, "It seems like I've been walking in the dark for months!"

Now the information that the focus person feels like she has been walking in the dark for months becomes part of the story, and the group begins responding to *that* reality as well, rather than bringing the focus person's attention back only to the original material. For example, "Your voice seemed full of emotion as you said you've spent months walking in the dark."

A certain asceticism is required from group members awaiting an opportunity to mention a different thread of the story, say, "Light-green new growth tipped each branch." In this case, they must simply let go of their initial responses, let go, but not forget, because the conversation may invite that contribution later in the process. For example, as the focus person finishes exploring the recent darkness of her life and mentions some positive events, a listener might remember his initial, unsaid response and feel prompted to mention the new growth tipping the branches in the midst of the dark woods.

Over a period of several days, the group listens contemplatively to each focus person for one hour and then spends fifteen minutes debriefing. During debriefing, the facilitator asks first the focus person and then the rest of the group to make observations about the rate and content of their responses, including which seemed most helpful and which seemed to fall flat. The facilitator also invites students to identify where they thought the heart of the matter was, what they experienced as they listened and responded, and where they sensed God's presence.

Implications of Contemplative Listening for Spiritual Direction

Contemplative listening involves receiving, making meaning, and responding: receiving the other, ourselves, and God; making meaning from what we hear; and responding in accordance with that meaning. In many ways, contemplative listening is the foundation that other spiritual direction skills are built upon. This is not lost on our students, and they call themselves and one another back to contemplative listening again and again throughout their years of training.

In spiritual direction, the practice of contemplative listening helps directors to make use of a wide range of their own perceptions as they seek to recognize God's sometimes subtle presence in addition to hearing their directees fully and well. Further, it provides a touchstone that directors can return to when they find themselves in challenging territory, say, when they notice that they're asking question after question, relying on advice giving, or feeling at a loss for what to say. By having recourse to contemplative listening, directors can refocus the conversation, leading it in a more fruitful direction. For example, they can check in with themselves to see what they are experiencing and respond out of that experience, or they can ask themselves where they notice God's presence and let that reality refresh them.

In addition, the process of learning contemplative listening helps students gain a felt sense of the wonder of contemplating a past event while attending to our experience in the present moment. That sets the stage for them to invite their directees to do the same, opening themselves to a present experience of God rather than remaining focused on the past.

Finally, when directors practice contemplative listening in their direction sessions, they train their directees by example to practice contemplative listening as well, a practice that has implications not only for direction sessions but for the rest of the directee's world. What better way to grow in faith, hope, and love, what surer way to experience our own transformation and that of the world than to notice and respond to God's presence in the course of our everyday lives and thus participate in the reign of God?

For Further Reflection

1. Recall a memory of being deeply heard. Share some of the qualities of such an experience.

2. What does it mean to receive the experience of another? How might you describe the skills needed for this type of listening?

3. What does it mean to respond to the experience of another? How might you describe the skills needed for this type of listening?

4. What skills come naturally for you? Which ones need more development?

Resources

Bowen, Maria Tattu. "Dimensions of Human Experience." In *Supervision of Spiritual Directors: Engaging in Holy Mystery,* ed. Mary Rose Bumpus and Rebecca Langer. Harrisburg, Pa.: Morehouse, 2005.

Burghardt, Walter J. "Contemplation: A Long, Loving, Look at the Real," *Church* (Winter 1989): 14–18.

Calvin, John. "The Knowledge of God and That of Ourselves Are Connected. How They Are Interrelated." In *Institutes of Christian Religion,* chapter 1, book 1, trans. Ford Lewis Battles, ed. John T. McNeill, 35–39. Philadelphia: Westminster Press, 1960.

Carr, Anne E. "Starting with the Human." In *A World of Grace: An Introduction to the Themes and Foundations of Karl Rahner's Theology*, ed. Leo J. O'Donovan, 17–30. Washington, D.C.: Georgetown University Press, 1995. (Originally published in 1980.)

Hart, Thomas. *The Art of Christian Listening.* Mahwah, N.J.: Paulist Press, 1980.

International Listening Association, 1996, *www.listen.org.*

May, Gerald. "Contemplative Presence." In *The Awakened Heart: Opening Yourself to the Love You Need,* 93–110. San Francisco: HarperSanFrancisco, 1991.

Patton, John. *From Ministry to Theology: Pastoral Action and Reflection.* Nashville: Abingdon Press, 1990.

Pritchard, Andrew. "Listening Ministry." In *Reality Magazine.* See online *www.reality.org.*

Taylor, Charles W. "Attending." In *The Skilled Pastor: Counseling as the Practice of Theology,* 15–30. Minneapolis: Fortress Press, 1991.

Weil, Simone, "Reflections on the Right Use of School Studies with a View to the Love of God," in *Waiting for God,* 57–66. New York: HarperCollins, 2001.

Journey in Faithfulness
Prayer and Spiritual Direction

Teresa of Ávila in *The Interior Castle* tells us that prayer is the door through which we must first step to begin in earnest our journey in faithfulness. The implication is clear: without prayer it is impossible to begin the journey to our deepest selves, the journey to God in whose image we have been created. John Calvin in the *Institutes of the Christian Religion* says that prayer is the chief exercise of faith. As such, it is one of the all-important acts in which a faithful believer must engage.

Prayer, *precatio* in Latin, means to entreat or to ask for something earnestly. The person who prays believes that God, the Divine Mystery of the universe, desires a relationship with the creature and creation. This divine and loving presence that transcends the bounds of human knowing welcomes us and wants to hear about our needs, our hopes, and our dreams. God so completely desires to be in relationship with us that we are created with a capacity to yearn for the Divine. In prayer, we spend time with God by opening ourselves to God's love and listening for God's call to be transformed.

Our best intentions toward the Divine, however, suffer when we become preoccupied with our own busyness. Nonetheless this God who "so loves the world" tugs and pulls, whispers and cajoles until we once again notice. We may respond with feelings of awe or puzzlement, with fear or questioning, or with sighs too deep for words. In each case the response is our prayer. It is our deepest and truest self responding to God's initiative. Stories about ourselves and the thick texture of these responses are often the content of spiritual direction conversations.

Types of Prayer

Faithfulness in prayer is faithfulness to the relationship with the Holy. This faithfulness takes many forms since different people have different ways of relating intimately to one another and to God. There is no one right way to pray, and there is no type of prayer that is superior to other types. What matters is that the prayer be a genuine expression of the relationship between the person, group or community, and God. Training programs will want to introduce future directors to a variety of forms of prayer so that they can appreciate the many ways relationships with the Holy are supported and sustained.

In my experience, those who come for spiritual direction training are frequently interested in learning more about praying with Scripture (for example, *lectio divina,* or the Four-Stranded Garland), Centering Prayer, and various types of prayers of *examen.* Others come having experienced the Jesus Prayer, body prayer, prayer with music, prayer using guided imagery, and action prayers for justice and peace. Providing opportunities for interns to engage in prayer during training sessions is indispensable. Here the learning involves both intellect and affect. Tending the Holy occurs both during the prayer and as participants share their sacred experiences in small groups. Those whose prayer has touched them at a profound level are enriched as they share with their peers. It is hoped such opportunities will deepen the interns' sensitivity to the Sacred and enhance their appreciation for the authentic experiences of others. Interns need to become comfortable listening to experiences of the Holy that differ from or seem more profound than their own.

Those training to become spiritual directors will want to be familiar with the literature about prayer. Providing interns with an introduction to often-used descriptors for prayer — that is, a prayer vocabulary — can include such terms as adoration, confession, thanksgiving, petition, kataphatic (praying with images or objects), apophatic (praying without images), meditative (pondering a biblical text, word, or image), and contemplative (resting in God with quiet openness).

Faithfulness to Prayer

Spiritual growth and transformation are not primarily fostered by a particular form of prayer, but by the intentional and disciplined practice of prayer. Although most people at times feel unworthy of a relationship with God, it is important to work through the resistance and continue to deepen this sacred relationship. To do this, three things are especially important. First, one must sincerely *desire* to respond to God's initiative. If we are seeking to enhance this relationship because we think we "should" or "ought" to draw closer to God, rather than because we sincerely desire this, we may unconsciously be using our relationship with God to enhance an idealized image of ourselves. If we truly desire a deeper relationship, we are more likely to be faithful in prayer. Second, we need to pray with regularity. That is, we need to be *disciplined* in our prayer life. This requires selecting a place, time, posture and method for prayer — often in consultation with a spiritual director — that is suitable to our personalities, lifestyles, and relationship with God. Such is the discipline not of the harsh disciplinarian, but of the dedicated runner or committed musician whose regular practice yields a transformation that remains elusive to the beginner. Third, we need a place for *accountability.* Being held accountable keeps us honest with ourselves and prevents us from excusing ourselves too easily when our discipline fails. This accountability comes from the compassionate support of a peer group, prayer group, or spiritual director. The warmth of their presence as they listen to us and raise questions about our desires and disciplines reminds us that God loves us and longs for us to return to prayer especially when we become preoccupied with our own agendas.

Prayer and the Directee

Some years ago when those seeking spiritual direction came primarily from the ordained and vowed religious communities of established faith traditions, it was assumed that they had active prayer lives or were consciously committed to deepening their relationship with God. Some who come for direction will be mature people of faith seeking a director who will help them listen for the movement of the Sacred in their lives. These directees may have experience with spiritual direction and have a sense of what they are seeking in a director. Others, however, may be less clear about their needs and expectations.

As the ministry of spiritual direction has gained attention in this postmodern, pluralistic culture, we can make few assumptions about those seeking direction. The director cannot assume that the directee knows much about prayer or has a relationship with the Divine. In my experience, some people come for spiritual guidance because they are looking for a deeper meaning to life than that which is offered by popular culture. Many contemporary seekers come for spiritual direction not because of the strength of their prayer life and their desire to examine its depths, but because of their longing for a relationship with the Sacred that seems beyond their grasp. Some have only a sense that something is missing in their lives. For these seekers, the quest begins not by opening the door to the castle or by the chief exercise of faith, but by their yearning and hope that there is a deeper significance to life than they have yet experienced. God, of course, is at work in that yearning. Today's spiritual directors hold the traditions of prayer and spiritual direction in one hand and the needs and experiences of those seeking direction in the other. Each is a gift from God.

Spiritual directors need to be able to teach basic prayer practices that are organically related to the lives of the directee. By this I mean that directors will want to help directees talk about what they do to nurture their spirits. Such activities may seem very secular, for example, jogging, playing an instrument, playing with a pet. As the director encourages the directee to speak about these experiences, the directee may discover a new depth in them. The directee learns to approach these activities with a new intentionality so that they have the potential to become avenues toward the Sacred. For example, routine exercise can becomes a conscious desire to respect the sacred nature of one's God-given body through its proper care. On the other hand, the joy of time with a pet can be transformed with intentionality from simple pleasure to a deep joy and appreciation for creation. Care for the body and time with the pet become avenues for seeing God's presence in everyday life. Simple prayers of gratitude or brief moments of quiet prayer for these experiences become the prayer that opens the castle door and deepens the relationship with God.

Prayer and the Spiritual Direction Session

Spiritual directors provide spiritual guidance to those seeking direction. This does not mean that directors dispense some form of holy directive or holy wisdom to their directees. Instead directors listen for the movement of God's Spirit in the lives of their directees. By listening carefully for the directee's affective interior movements and for the significant aspects of the directee's narrative, the director invites the directee to notice how God is present. The focus during their time together is on the directee's relationship with the Divine.

As directees tell their stories, raise questions, and experience joy or pain, the direction session itself may become a prayer. The director and the directee's conversation moves to a profound place where they come to realize they are "standing" on holy ground. Directors are trained to sense this sacred ground and to honor it by helping their directees notice it themselves. Often when we touch the Sacred, we have a tendency to flee from this deep place. It may not feel comfortable to us if we have not been there often. Or it may frighten us because we fear what might be asked of us. Being in the presence of the Holy with someone we trust can help us deepen our relationship with the Divine.

Spiritual directors often adapt their use of prayer during a session to the wishes and needs of the directee. While some directees are familiar with prayer and appreciate directors who open or close a session with prayer, directees who have had little religious formation may not be comfortable with verbal prayers. Many directors report that they use the symbol system or language their directees prefer especially in initial sessions. If it becomes appropriate to teach prayer practices, directors may introduce prayer forms from their religious traditions. Directors who do not pray aloud with their directees may provide a time for silent prayer. Such time allows people from diverse faith traditions or those with more secular formation to use the silence in ways that are personally meaningful.

Prayer tables or small worship centers with a candle, Bible, fresh flowers, art work, icon, or other devotional objects are normally present in the meeting rooms of spiritual directors. These objects remind both the director and directee that they are in the presence of the Holy and that it is the Holy Spirit who truly is the director in both their lives. This attention to prayer and devotion provides a context that is safe and welcoming for discussing the directee's concerns.

Prayer and the Spiritual Director

Those who provide spiritual guidance need themselves to be people of prayer. If directors are trained to notice the Holy and help their directees tend the Holy, they also must be faithful to their relationship with God. This means that spiritual directors should continue to be in direction themselves in order to keep noticing their own interior movements and the work of God in their lives. For most, this means engaging with intention in a variety of spiritual practices, including prayer.

In the process of spiritual direction is it expected that directees will have questions about their own responses to God and to the existential events in their lives. When these situations are difficult, a directee may wonder whether God cares for them, or whether God can accept their anger, doubt, or fear. Spiritual directors frequently ask the directee if they have taken their concern to prayer. Often we may forget to take our concerns to prayer. Being reminded by the director that this is helpful and necessary is often experienced as a grace. Directors need this guidance and experience from their own direction sessions to offer it to others. This experience of a graced encounter with the director that points to the relationship of prayer with the Divine around a concrete issue or concern in a directee's life must be experienced to be profoundly understood. Directors need to know at an experiential level the dynamics of this experience if they are to serve as guides for others.

Praying at regular intervals for one's directees is an important discipline for spiritual directors. This may involve petitionary prayer for particular needs the directee has surfaced in conversation with the director or it may be as simple as the director holding the directee in the light of God's healing presence. Spiritual directors are people of prayer who come from communities and congregations of faith that affirm the work of God's transforming love in all the world. As a result, directors routinely incorporate their concern for their directees into their daily prayer life.

Growth in Prayer

As our relationship with God changes over time, so can the form or type of prayer that we find meaningful. When these changes are occurring, the guidance and support of a spiritual director can be especially helpful. Prayer forms that have been meaningful may become dry regardless of how sincerely they have been practiced. This may seem especially perplexing for those who have had a rich experiential relationship with the Holy where consolations and solace were familiar. Directees may fear that they have done something wrong and are no longer worthy. After careful companioning and listening where both the director and the directee honor what is happening for the directee, spiritual directors need to be able to offer alternative prayer forms for those who simply need something enlivening. Relationships change, and when they change new means of communicating may be required. Some directees may find learning a new prayer practice or going back to a former prayer discipline will be helpful. However, the good director does not try to fix the directee's prayer by quickly offering new ways to pray. The director may gently affirm that the directee's experiential relationship with the Holy is changing. The director who believes that a new prayer form might be helpful will also carefully listen to the movement of the Spirit to decide when it would be right to introduce this suggestion. If the directee is responsive, the director should be able to provide the instruction necessary.

The director also needs to be comfortable helping the directee stay with a particularly arid period that may be a dark night. The directee may be entering a period where prayer with consolation is gone and faith alone is the anchor. Suggesting new forms of prayer at this point would be inappropriate. Instead, the steady attentiveness of the director will be especially valued during this time when directees are particularly vulnerable.

Experienced directors will also note that for people who have prayed for many years there may come a time when most formal prayer forms seem inadequate or drop away. There may be a spontaneity to prayer or an internalizing of one's relationship with the Holy that seems as natural as breathing. Directors who have not experienced this in their own prayer lives may mistakenly try to provide new prayer forms for directees who have outgrown them. This quiet and profound internalization of God's presence allows the directee to look with the eyes of God and respond to the needs of the world with compassion and justice. Whether this prayer takes the form of spontaneously "practicing the presence" of God or "a union with God," as many of the saints have said, it must be honored by the director. Here the director can help the directee identify and celebrate that which the director may not have experienced.

For Further Reflection

1. Do you find it helpful to think about prayer as a place where your relationship with God is nurtured? If so, what is helpful? What new thoughts if any arise?

2. How would you describe your prayer? What forms do you use?

3. Are you comfortable talking about your prayer life? Have you shared aspects of your prayer with your spiritual director? What impact has this had (a) on your prayer, (b) on your spiritual direction sessions?

4. What qualities do you think are developed by being a person of prayer? Do you see these in your director? How does this help you as the directee?

🌸 Resources

Calvin, John. *John Calvin: Writings on Pastoral Piety.* Edited and trans. Elsie Anne McKee. Mahwah, N.J.: Paulist Press, 2002.

Dossey, Larry. *Healing Words: The Power of Prayer and the Practice of Medicine.* San Francisco: HarperSanFrancisco, 1993.

Foster, Richard. *Finding the Heart's True Home.* San Francisco: HarperSanFrancisco, 1992.

Job, Rueben, and Norm Sawchuck. *A Guide to Prayer for All God's People.* Nashville: Upper Room, 1990.

Keating, Thomas. *Foundations for Centering Prayer and Christian Contemplative Life: Open Mind, Open Heart, Invitation to Love, Mystery of Christ.* New York: Continuum, 2002.

Pennington, M. Basil. *Lectio Divina: Renewing the Ancient Practice of Praying the Scriptures.* New York: Crossroad, 1998.

Steere, Douglas. *Dimensions of Prayer: Cultivating a Relationship with God.* Nashville: Upper Room, 1997.

Teresa of Ávila. *Interior Castle.* Trans. and ed. E. Allision Peers. New York: Image Books, 1961.

Thompson, Marjorie J. *Soul Feast: An Invitation to the Christian Spiritual Life.* Louisville: Westminster/John Knox Press, 1995.

Thurman, Howard. *With Head and Heart.* New York: Harcourt Brace Jovanovich, 1981.

Presence: The Journal of Spiritual Directors International. Published three
   times a year.
Spiritus: A Journal of Christian Spirituality. Published twice a year by
   The Johns Hopkins University Press.

Waiting on God
Staying with Movements of God

The major premises that underlie spiritual direction are disarmingly simple, namely, that God is active in our lives, constantly taking the initiative; that God's actions are unrelentingly loving (which is not to say always easy or comforting but, rather, always on the side of our deepest desires); that we can experience these actions of God, can sense the movements of God's Spirit; and that we can respond to these movements either with willingness or with resistance.

Spiritual direction at its best entirely focuses on helping the directee to become attentive to the presence, action, and movements of God in ordinary human experiences, and on noticing the directee's own responses to these movements of the Holy. Whatever content the direction conversation may hold, however many interesting twists and turns and diverse paths it takes, the director listens for one thing only. The director "tunes in" like a person fiddling carefully with a radio dial, spinning from one music clip to another, one fragment of speech to the next, until "Aha, this is it!" The director recognizes the presence of God in the conversation and then helps the directee to explore further what has occurred or is occurring.

Attending to God's Movements

It follows, then, that we as spiritual directors must be people "poised unto the Holy," to use the words of Brian McDermott, SJ,[6] sufficiently practiced in God's ways to notice God's actions in the life of our directee. How, precisely, do we recognize these experiences of God? We recognize them by noticing what evokes an unmistakable resonance in our own hearts, by what is immediately and deeply attractive to us. This "resonance" is akin to the synchronicity of lovers whom Rilke describes in his poem "Liebeslied" (Love Song). Alluding to the fact that, when one string is played on a musical instrument, the strings an octave higher or lower will also vibrate, Rilke writes: "Everything that touches us, you and me, takes us together as a bow's stroke does, that out of two strings draws a single voice."

If we are attentive, we literally experience a similar stirring in the presence of God, and in the telling of the God-story by the directee. No amount of theological training or programs in spiritual direction can ever substitute for the surrendered heart that maintains such a contemplative stance, always with an ear toward God's sweet song — or at least toward the sometimes dim memory of it. Like the commercials that warn, "Do not try this at home," we should not attempt the ministry of spiritual direction without first having been honed and humbled by years of prayerful waiting on God. Walter Burghardt calls contemplation "a long, loving look at the real."[7] Without such a steady, earthy, open, welcoming embrace of life, spiritual direction is impossible.

So how do we become attuned to the movements of God in human experience? There is precious little in our culture that supports such a stance. Our culture does not value stopping, waiting, noticing, or pondering, though all of these are required for prayer. Our culture questions fidelity, disparages suffering, and cannot even imagine turning one's cheek or loving an enemy. Yet these, if the Scriptures are to be believed, are precisely the ways of God. Our culture locks doors to keep out strangers and hoards resources for rainy days. Yet God comes in the guise of a stranger and laughs at those who build bigger barns. Our culture takes pains to reward good deeds and punish evildoing, yet God persists in being extravagantly generous and forgiving, upending all our ideas of what is fair. Our culture lauds talent and success, yet God chooses to identify with "the least among us."

Discerning God's Movements

Spiritual direction requires that we — director and directee — recognize that our ways are often not God's ways. We must nurture a willingness to be divested, day by day, of anything that contradicts the ways of God. This is what Ignatius meant by discernment, and this is the work of the director: deliberately sifting through the grist of each day — our feelings, inclinations, attractions, repugnance, our choices or avoidance of choices, our moments of consolation and our times of desolation — seeking to identify what aligns us with God and what pulls us away from God.

There is an inspirational story about a tribal elder who described his own inner struggles in this manner: "Inside of me there are two dogs. One of the dogs is mean and evil. The other dog is good. The mean dog fights the good dog all the time." When asked which dog wins, he reflected for a moment and replied, "The one I feed the most."[8] We can think of spiritual direction as the care and feeding of the "good dog," of our deepest inner desires for goodness, our yearning for God.

It may be true that "the devil is in the details," but God is most certainly there too. Spiritual direction disciplines us to pay attention to the details where God dwells, because what we pay attention to, grows. Again, our culture does not help us much here. We've been brought up to expect God in an otherworldly realm: in thunderbolts or angels or the "final rapture" rather than in the laughter of children, the pain of an addiction, a relationship gone wrong, or the restlessness within us that nothing seems to satisfy. When insurance companies speak of "acts of God," they are referring to earthquakes and tsunamis, not to spring blossoms or unexpected kindnesses. In Scripture, however, we see a God who prefers hiddenness, a God delighting in mercy, a God close to the brokenhearted. So when we tend the hidden parts of ourselves, or allow forgiveness to take root in our hearts, or sit patiently with those who grieve, we are likely to come astonishingly close to God. Spiritual direction exists to help us notice these very human and almost mundane "close encounters" —

or their absence — and to ask where God is at work (or at play) in them right now.

Following the Fork in the Road

My colleagues and I often use the image of the fork in the road. By this we mean a point in the direction conversation where the director can follow one of two diverging paths. The path we take, to paraphrase Robert Frost, "makes all the difference." It is our responsibility always to track, first and foremost, the directee's human experience of God. The direction session is never merely casual conversation; the director makes a commitment to stay with the exploration of movements of God. This makes all the difference. Let's now look at some examples of how we can listen for the experience of God in the direction conversation, help the directee to stay with and explore that experience rather than move away from it, and then attend to its effects in the life of the directee in future sessions. Consider the following two scenarios.

Scenario 1: The Gardener with a Bible

The directee says, "I find that gardening is a wholesome release for me on the weekends, but I've been wanting to learn from you how to pray the Scriptures." This is a "fork moment," a moment to discern. As directors, we have a clear choice: to pursue the affective sense of release that the directee experiences in gardening, or to jump at the chance to teach the directee how to prayer from Scripture. Watch how differently the conversation unfolds, depending on the choice.

1. The Bible Fork

Directee: I find that gardening is a wholesome release for me on the weekends, but I've been wanting to learn from you how to pray the Scriptures.

Director: Gardening is wonderful. But you're right, you have asked me before about praying the Scriptures, and I see you've brought your Bible today.

Directee: Yes, last month when you prayed aloud for me at the end of our session, I recognized a few snatches from the Psalms. Is that a good place to start, with the Psalms?

Director: Many people do find them to be a natural starting place.

Directee: Is there an particular one I should use?

Director: Well, it depends on how you are feeling. Psalm 23, if you're feeling lost; Psalm 51 if you seek God's forgiveness, for example.

Directee: Hmmm. Should I just read them slowly?

Director: I recommend reading one Psalm slowly, then pausing to let the sentiments sink in. If one line, or even one word, attracts you, you can sit with that a while, and talk it over with God.

Directee: That really appeals to me.

Director: Try it and we can talk about it next month.

2. The Gardener Fork

Directee: I find that gardening is a wholesome release for me on the weekends, but I've been wanting to learn from you how to pray the Scriptures.

Director: Uh-hunh. Tell me more about that sense of release.

Directee: Well, it just feels good to get my hands into the soil and pull up the weeds and make it possible for seeds to sprout.

Director: Yes, it can be very relaxing.

Directee: Totally, and then after an hour or two of messing around in the back yard, I find that I can be more patient with the kids; things don't get on my nerves as much. Almost as if I'm a better person.

Director: Tell me more about that.

Directee:[Pause.] Maybe I'm finally believing, after all these years of being so uptight and trying to be perfect, that God is tending me, and weeding me, and actually rejoicing in the signs of new life in me.

Director: So, what's it like to feel that God is tending you?

Scenario 2: The Volunteer Who Felt Empty

Here the "fork" appears when the directee mentions that he has started to volunteer in response to the emptiness he feels since the death of his wife.

1. The Volunteer Fork

Directee: I've been volunteering at the parish soup kitchen every Wednesday morning. It really helps me to not feel so empty since Marie died.

Director: So you're reaching out despite your own pain.

Directee: I try to. It isn't easy. I always think that Marie would be pleased.

Director: Tell me about that.

Directee: Oh, she was a joiner — always helping out with some women's club or church activity. Amazing how it seemed to give her energy.

Directee: So are you volunteering to honor her memory?

Directee: That could be what it is, I suppose. Mainly I'm just trying not to get stuck in my own grieving.

Director: Do you feel stuck?

Directee: Not really. Just feeling alone.

2. The Emptiness Fork

Directee: I've been volunteering at the parish soup kitchen every Wednesday morning. It really helps me to not feel so empty since Marie died.

Director: Her death left a big hole in your life.

Directee: That doesn't even begin to describe it. A hole has a bottom. But this feeling is just endlessly empty.

Director: Tell me about the emptiness.

Directee: Well, the funny thing is, I've always thought of God as a presence. Just like Marie was always present, always at my side. But since the day she died, I've missed her so much that I've begun to think of both her and God as absences in my life. Like black holes.

Director: Where something beloved used to be?

Directee: Yes, and I feel strangely drawn to the holes. Just to sit there next to what used to be, and ache for it.

Director: [Pause] A longing?

Directee: I find myself sitting in my big chair every night, feeling pulled into the absences, and letting myself be pulled there. Other stuff drops away, it's just me and the absences. And afterward, I feel more loving. Hard to explain. But that's why I started helping out at the soup kitchen. I just had to express it somehow.

In all of these scenarios, the director is a good listener; in all, the director tends to the human experience and elicits more detail. But there is a striking difference in both examples when the director chooses the fork that has hinted at the directee's experience of God, and thus has triggered in the director a desire to hear more. Sometimes these experiences of God are fleeting, uncertain, or even disturbing. The directee can all too readily resist or dismiss his or her experience of God. We are not always comfortable staying with our deepest feelings or praying from that place.

When we are discerning clearly, we bring the conversation back to the point of revelation by guiding the directee to stay with each movement, to name it, and to follow it. Grace, after all, is not some mysterious substance that, depending on our actions, we get more of or less of throughout our life. Grace is the word we use to refer to our relationship with God. It is everything that strengthens that friendship, including setbacks. Nothing is ever lost. All of it makes up who we are now and who we are becoming in God's sight.

One method for helping directees to name their experiences of God is to encourage concreteness. We should never assume as a director that we know what the directee means. If a directee says, "Nothing happens in my prayer," ask for greater detail. "What do you mean by 'nothing'?" or "What fills the minutes?" or "What happens when you're there?" You may be surprised at what you learn! When a directee says, "God is like the fog," does he mean God is a quiet, mysterious presence, or a bone-chilling darkness impossible to penetrate? When a directee speaks of being comforted by God, does she mean feeling embraced, or being braced to stand strong? We cannot know unless we ask the directee to be more specific. This helps the directee (whose experiences may be inchoate or preverbal) to understand how and where God is active.

It is natural to resist anything that threatens the status quo. Since God is always leading us toward becoming more loving, we will often resist God's approach. As directors, our role is to explore these movements with the directee until there is clarity, and freedom for choice. God is always so much more than we can expect or imagine. In plumbing our daily human experience, we encounter the living God. As directors, we help our directees to explore and respond to those encounters — and in the process, we too are transformed. What could ever be more privileged, more demanding, more life-affirming, than this ministry?

For Further Reflection

1. What might it mean for me, concretely, to be "poised unto the Holy"?

2. What does it mean to say that "God is in the details"?

3. When have I felt with another person, to use Rilke's words, a shared sweet song?

4. What kinds of "fork moments" do I recognize in my own direction narrative?

 ## Resources

Barry, William A., and William J. Connolly, *The Practice of Spiritual Direction.* San Francisco: HarperSanFrancisco, 1982.

Edwards, Denis. *Human Experience of God.* Mahwah, N.J.: Paulist Press, 1983.

Edwards, Tilden. *Spiritual Director/Spiritual Companion: Guide to Tending the Soul.* Mahwah, N.J.: Paulist Press, 2001.

Houdek, Frank, SJ. *Guided By the Spirit.* Chicago: Loyola University Press, 1996.

Running from God

Resistance to the Movements of God[9]

One of the blessings of our time has been the rediscovery of the ever-dynamic presence of God's Spirit sustaining all that is. Far from the image of "Unmoved Mover" promoted by theologians in centuries past — a distant divinity moving chess pieces on a giant playing field — we understand that God is intimately bound up with our lives and our longings. The God whom the Scriptures describe as Lover, Mother, Father of the Prodigal, Healer, Shepherd, Breath, and Song stands always at our door, ready to be welcomed in. This God invites us, woos us, desires our company. The prophets even speak of being "seduced" by the attractiveness of God.[10] For a seeker who "finds God" (or is found by God), the experience can be akin to falling in love, with all the giddy abandonment and extravagance love entails.

Evasion of God

As spiritual directors we will see this kind of movement in our directees. It is certainly reason for rejoicing! But over time, we will also see that the human heart *resists* this Love, skirts it, moves away from it, and even denies any experience of it. What accounts for such seemingly contrary behavior? Why would we resist the very One for whom our hearts long? The reason, of course, is simple: Love changes us. Love summons us to grow into the Beloved. And such change — religious tradition calls it "conversion" — threatens the self we identify with and cling to with all our might. When God draws near, we may initially feel consoled, but soon we will discover that God is also a consuming fire, a hammer shattering rock.[11] "No one can see me

61

and live,"[12] Yahweh warns Moses. God's ways are not our ways, as Deutero-Isaiah notes.[13] Taking a path toward God inevitably means leaving behind much that we hold dear.

When we commit ourselves to God's ways, we discover that Love pulls us beyond our comfort zones and into a world where, despite overwhelming appearances to the contrary, love does unite all beings. This is, as Belden Lane describes in *The Solace of Fierce Landscapes,* not necessarily an easy place to be: "Yahweh frequently moves the boundary in order to restore the center, calling a broken people back to justice and compassion. Jesus, in a similar way, frequently presses the people closest to him into places they find threatening. He functions repeatedly as a boundary crosser, pushing his disciples to edges they find exceedingly uncomfortable."[14]

Thus it should not surprise us that the human heart displays remarkable ingenuity, often at an unconscious level, in evading the consequences of encountering God.[15] Divine intimacy can be powerfully appealing and yet frightening at the same time. We find marvelous ways to distract ourselves from it. I have a colleague who admits that every time she senses God drawing near, she gets up and busies herself with watering the plants in her house! Eight centuries ago, the Sufi poet Rumi marveled at his own ambivalence in the face of what he most desired. Much of his poetry reflects his own journey in which he resisted the insistence of God, desiring to live within Love, yet running away.

Manifestations of Resistance

My colleagues and I spend considerable time with our interns exploring this phenomenon of resistance, since the place of resistance signals the place where God is active, where the directee's transformation can occur.[16] Resistance shows itself in many ways and is psychologically complex.[17]

+ Sometimes a directee will deny his or her experiences of God: "Oh, that was just emotion — my own projection of a need to feel loved."

- Sometimes there will be literal repression: on a subsequent visit the directee will have no recollection of an experience of, for example, consolation that was described in great detail the previous month. If we prompt the directee to recall it, he or she may give it a vague dismissal, indicating that the directee is completely out of touch with the affective content of the experience: "Did I say that? Well, I don't think it was that important; it was just a passing thing."

- Sometimes the directee intellectualizes the experience to keep it at arm's length: "Yes, I did initially feel inclined to forgive Jean for what she said about me, but then I realized that it would be better to hold her accountable for being so hurtful. She needs to learn that it isn't right to go around ruining people's reputations like that."

- Sometimes the directee will transfer his or her resistance onto us: "Sit with these feelings of longing when I pray? No, I don't think that makes any sense. I tried it and ended up stuck in erotic daydreams. I know it's not possible for you to always understand me."

- Sometimes the directee simply dodges the conversion point altogether, and actually keeps it a secret from us: "What does God desire for me? Hmm, no, I have no sense of anything. My prayer is just sort of ordinary."

- Sometimes the directee sidesteps our questions, steers the conversation away from certain areas, or responds with "I don't know."

- Sometimes the directee displaces the longing for God elsewhere, turning to an addiction, perhaps, or other pursuits to slake the underlying thirst, while keeping God "frozen" in a certain image that protects him or her from meaningful encounter: "I just can't pray to a God that is male. Serving the poor is now my way of praying."

- Sometimes the directee shifts from first-person dialogue to third-person narrative. This often indicates a need to distance him- or herself from the experience of God: "People should expect that there will be times in their lives when God isn't really active, right?"

- And sometimes the directee makes a conscious choice to turn away from God's presence, realizing that allowing God "in" may cost too dearly. Like Dietrich Bonhoeffer, the directee may be painfully aware that there is no such thing as "cheap grace," no chance of enjoying the presence of God without following this great Love all the way to the cross: "I have this growing awareness that staying with my job at the weapons factory contributes to the oppression of the poor. But I just can't leave! I have seniority there and a high salary. After all, I'm responsible for my family."

Interestingly, we directors can also sense resistance in the directee by tending to own inner affect. When the direction conversation goes "flat," there is a lessening of personal engagement. The God-narrative within the direction conversation is deeply attractive, and when it is absent or suppressed, the director feels bored, disconnected.

Learning from Resistance

Resistance, after all, is a healthy sign. It means something is happening. God is passing by. Love is beckoning, calling us to "lose our lives in order to find them."[18] Sometimes in the midst of the direction session, the directee's desiring self and resisting self meet. This is a delicate moment, one that we must attend to carefully. Most human beings will instinctively react to any such perceived threat to their self-image by "circling the wagons" and trying to preserve the status quo. Love, however, knows that the way to union passes through self-emptying, even to the point of losing everything, including the Beloved.[19]

When we recognize resistance in any of its many guises, our role is to help the directee to notice what is happening, to name it, and especially to track when the movement away from God began. It is never a matter of pointing out that the directee is resisting God. Rather, we encourage the directee to reflect back in time to discover that point when his or her affect shifted, when the engagement with God seemed to change or disappear. In a supportive context, we need never use the word "resistance," because the directee can often discover the block.

Let's see how this might unfold in the midst of an actual direction session.

Directee: There really isn't much happening in my life or my prayer right now. I'm doing okay at work these days; a bit less stressed now that the budget cycle is settled. . . .

Director: Mmm-hmmm. Nothing worth talking about?

Directee: No, I'm just kind of bored at prayer. The meditation hour seems to drag, actually.

Director: I recall that last month you described your experience when praying "the vine and the branches"[20] after having been to the wine country in Napa with your wife.

Directee: Oh, that. Yes, I guess I exaggerated a bit. It was my first time to see grapevines growing.

Director: Exaggerated?

Directee: Well, yes, I think I told you how impressed I was by the way the vines and the branches were curled so tightly around each other. I was startled by that, and couldn't help but think of the analogy that Jesus used in the Gospel.

Director: I recall your tears when you spoke of that relationship — how moved you were by realizing that Jesus wants you to cling that tightly to him.

Directee: That's what I mean by exaggerating. I got a little emotional about it. I'm beyond that now.

Director: Beyond it?

Directee: Yes, I recognize that it was a figure of speech. What God really wants is for me to live a good life and care for my family. And I am trying to do that as best as I can every day.

Director: But your prayer is boring now? It drags?

Directee: Yes.

Director: Do you recall when that started? It wasn't that way after you were in Napa....

Directee: Oh, it's been kind of dull for a few weeks now.

Director: Did anything shift in you? Can you remember when it might have changed?

Directee: [Long silence.] Well, now that you ask, I do recall feeling kind of embarrassed by the feeling that Jesus desired a real closeness with me and what that might mean. The image of those intertwined vines and branches — it was so vivid! I even went on the Internet and printed out a photo of a vineyard and put it on my desk at work. For a few days, I felt very happy, but then the whole idea somehow seemed silly, and a little scary. So I tossed the picture and got back to my normal way of praying.

In this brief excerpt from a direction session, the director's gentle but focused questioning has helped the directee to retrace his steps until he reached a point of insight about precisely when and how the he had moved away from God's invitation to intimacy, for fear of its implications in his life.

The presence of resistance usually indicates that God is at work. As skilled directors, therefore, we pay attention to it and treat it as an opportunity for the directee to grow in understanding how God is acting in his or her life, and how we must learn, as William Blake poetically says, "to bear the beams of love."[21]

 ## For Further Reflection

1. What patterns of resistance to God have you noticed in your faith journey?

2. It has been said that "Resistance is the dragon that guards the treasure." What image do you have of resistance in the spiritual direction process?

3. What has been helpful to you as a directee when resistance has surfaced in the direction session?

4. What type of resistance might be most challenging to you as a director? Explain.

Resources

Barry, William A., and William J. Connolly . *The Practice of Spiritual Direction.* San Francisco: HarperSanFrancisco, 1982.

May, Gerald. *Care of Mind, Care of Spirit.* San Francisco: HarperSan-Francisco, 1982.

Ruffing, Janet. *Spiritual Direction: Beyond the Beginnings.* Mahwah, N.J.: Paulist Press, 2000.

Soelle, Dorothee. *The Silent Cry: Mysticism and Resistance,* translated by Barbara and Martin Rumscheidt. Minneapolis: Fortress Press, 2001.

OPEN TO
THE MYSTERY

Toward Union with God

Development and Transitions in Prayer

Familiarity with the major stages and transitions in prayer is an important component in the formation of spiritual directors. It can provide us with a basic sense of orientation in our work and help us to listen in a more appreciative and discerning way to the experience of directees. A broad perspective on the journey of prayer can open us as directors to a spectrum of possibilities beyond what we may have personally experienced and free us to respond with greater flexibility to the changing prayer experiences of directees.

Developmental approaches to prayer also carry some risks. If we are insecure in our role as directors, a superficial grasp of classic and contemporary maps of the spiritual journey may give us the illusion that possession of a map will give us a handle on the Mystery. We may lose focus by attempting to anxiously figure out what stage directees have reached rather than exploring with them in depth their unique experiences of God.

Maps of spiritual development, though valid and useful, need to be held lightly when we engage the actual prayer experiences of directees. Prayer resists facile reduction to typical patterns. It involves the intersection of God's freedom and human freedom, an essentially creative and unpredictable encounter in which exceptions to the norm are the rule. As we read in John 3:8, "The wind blows where it wills . . . but you do not know where it comes from or where it goes. . . ."

Beginning with Experience

In exploring development in prayer in formation classes, it is important for participants to ground themselves in the particulars of their
own spiritual history. This can be done through exercises involving
art, movement, guided meditation, journaling, or other approaches
that allow participants to get a felt sense of their relationship with
God over time. Once the overall flow of the relationship has been
experienced and explored, the principal phases or stages of the journey can be distinguished in whatever ways seem most appropriate to
the individual. Finally, participants can be invited to listen contemplatively for a "master metaphor" that captures the quality of their
journey in prayer as a whole. Examples of some traditional master
metaphors of spiritual development include ascent of a mountain,
an inner journey to the center of a temple or palace, a battle between
forces of good and evil, a quest for a sacred treasure, a love affair
between the soul and God, appropriation of key events in the life of
a spiritual leader, the organic growth of a plant or flower, awakening from sleep, and liberation from captivity. Participants should be
encouraged to find their own metaphors and not feel bound by these
examples from the world's wisdom traditions.

When this exercise is complete, participants are invited to share
their reflections with one another in dyads. Those in the role of listener are encouraged to listen not simply to what is said, but to the
way their partner imagines the journey and to the tone and style
of his or her unique relationship with God. After each person has
shared and listened in dyads, the whole group gathers to process the
exercise. This discussion tends to bring to light both the variety and
commonality in the developmental prayer journeys of participants.
Individuals sense connections between their own journeys and those
of others in the group despite the diversity of master metaphors and
the uniqueness of each person's relationship with God.

This exercise can be extended following the class through a reflection paper in which participants are invited to explore more deeply
the phases of their relationship with God in the light of the master

metaphor that emerged in meditation. This kind of reflection is valuable preparation for spiritual direction which involves at its core exploration of the experiences that constitute a directee's unfolding spiritual journey.

The Interior Castle:
A Classic Map of the Journey of Prayer

These grounding exercises give participants a personal reference point as they approach maps of development in prayer drawn from the history of spirituality. There are many possible maps from which to choose, but I have found that Teresa of Ávila's classic work *The Interior Castle* is a particularly comprehensive and accessible account of the Christian journey of prayer.[22]

Teresa of Ávila was a sixteenth-century mystic, spiritual writer, and reformer of the Carmelite order in her native Spain. *The Interior Castle* was written toward the end of her life and is considered the mature synthesis of her teaching on prayer. The master metaphor that Teresa employs in *The Interior Castle* is the image of the human soul as a transparent crystal castle in which God dwells at the center as a source of radiant light. The journey of prayer consists in exploring ever more deeply the various rooms of the castle on the way to union with God at the center. Teresa groups the rooms of the castle into seven principal realms, though she makes clear that the journey is not a simple linear progression. One can move in and out, up and down, freely exploring new rooms and revisiting old rooms previously entered.

The Journey from Worldly to Religious Values

Teresa begins the journey with a description of the first rooms of prayer in which individuals are still quite caught up in attachment to possessions, pleasure, and social acceptance. Such persons "sometimes pray, but their minds are then filled with business matters that ordinarily occupy them."[23] Their prayer tends to be hurried, sporadic, and focused more on self than God. However, these brief moments of prayer begin to open a way into the castle by awakening deeper self-knowledge and a desire for a more faithful relationship with God.

In the second rooms, individuals begin to exert more effort but still lack determination and discipline. God ordinarily reaches them through external means such as books, sermons, and spiritual conversations. At this stage there is still quite a bit of ambivalence about embracing the spiritual life, and much time and effort in prayer is spent motivating oneself with reasons why one should pray in the face of resistance, laziness, and vulnerability to distractions.

In the third rooms, individuals have succeeded in becoming reasonable and responsible people who live in a well-ordered way. They are fond of prayer and self-discipline, and are "balanced in speech and dress and in the governing of their households."[24] The prayer of people at this stage tends to express itself in external practices and the active use of reason and imagination in meditation. People at this stage are typically more concerned with law and letter rather than grace and spirit. "Love," Teresa notes, "has not yet reached the point of overwhelming reason."[25]

There is a shadow side to all this righteous behavior. Teresa observes that people in the third rooms are overly disturbed by their own faults and tend to be introspectively preoccupied with how they feel in prayer. "They canonize these feelings in their minds and would like others to do so."[26] They also tend to be judgmental of others and are "shocked by everything."[27] The portrait that emerges is that of individuals whose external behavior is clearly oriented toward religious values and concerns, but whose egos are still very much in control.

The Cocoon of Transformation and the Night of the Senses

In the last four groups of rooms of the castle, the ego control that characterizes the first three groups begins to give way to ever deeper surrender to God's transforming action. Prayer relies less on active use of reason and imagination and more on quiet awareness of God's presence deep in the core of one's being. In the fourth rooms, Teresa emphasizes the positive side of this emergence of contemplation. She focuses her attention on the increase in love, freedom, trust, interior delight, and peace that are the fruits of this transition.

The emergence of affective and contemplative experiences in the fourth rooms gradually leads to a fundamental and often painful breakthrough in the fifth rooms. Teresa compares the transformation involved to a silkworm spinning a cocoon in which it dies to its former caterpillar way of life. The God-initiated prayer in the fifth rooms takes place in the dark, at a deep level that cannot be grasped by ordinary sense perception and thought. Prayer in the cocoon requires radical surrender to a God of Mystery whom one can neither rationally understand nor control. This is the reason why John of the Cross, Teresa's friend and collaborator in the Carmelite reform, called this transition a "night of the senses."

John notes that this dark transition to a contemplative mode of being is distinguished by three signs.[28] The first sign is the experience of enduring and pervasive dryness and dissatisfaction in prayer and life. The rational, well-ordered ways of relating to God and others that characterized the third rooms now feel superficial, empty, in disarray. The Spirit is still alive and active at deep interior levels of experience, but individuals in this transition are not yet spiritually attuned to the finer, subtle qualities of Divine presence that are now emerging. They remain restless, unsatisfied, and incapable of clearly grasping what is happening.

The second sign is the reluctant recognition that one does not really want to return to the old ways.[29] There is a disinclination to think and strive in prayer and life with the focused use of reason, imagination, and will that marked earlier stages. Acknowledging this lack of desire can be frightening at first. It feels like one is backsliding, failing to do what one *should* be doing. It is not unusual for people to anxiously exert extra effort at the old familiar methods of prayer for a while, but ultimately these attempts are recognized as futile and unsatisfying.

The third and surest sign is that one desires "to remain alone in loving awareness of God . . . in interior and quiet and repose."[30] The individual just wants to be with God, to rest in the love of God below the level of rational thought and anxious striving. This simple, loving attention is the actual experience of contemplation.

Both Teresa and John recognize that the transition to contemplative prayer involves a death or surrender of the old self and its habitual modes of operating: "One should let the intellect go and surrender into the arms of love."[31] The new self that emerges from the darkness of the cocoon of transformation has the capacity to intuit Spirit directly with an inner eye of love that operates beyond the reach of normal ego faculties.

The Night of Spirit and Union with God

Teresa's description of the sixth rooms of prayer is by far the longest and most detailed chapter in *The Interior Castle*. She places many of the experiences commonly identified with mystical prayer in these rooms: ecstasies, visions, inner words, direct spiritual intuitions, and intense spiritual longings. These phenomena appear to be byproducts of the transformation process and occur in some but not all people as they move deeper into contemplative prayer. Teresa is careful to point out that these phenomena can easily lead to self-deception and grandiosity if one is not firmly grounded in humility and the ordinary forms of loving one's neighbor. The criteria that Teresa formulates for discerning true from false religious experiences in the sixth rooms can still be of practical value to directors today.

Teresa and John note that before the individual realizes full union with God, interior and exterior suffering often increase as the last vestiges of the old self die and the new God-centered self emerges into consciousness. The roots of the old self are exposed and transformed through patient endurance of inner and outer conflicts, disillusionments, failures, and the emergence of unhealed wounds from the past. The deepest source of pain is the revolution that is occurring in one's relationship with God. Conventional beliefs and images of God are relentlessly stripped away or revealed as inadequate. Intimacy with God intensifies to such a degree that barriers between God and self begin to dissolve. The transformation that began in the night of the senses is here brought to completion in a deeper and more thorough purification that John of the Cross calls the night of the spirit.

The culmination of the transformation process is deep and permanent union with God in the seventh and central room of the castle. Teresa compares this union to what happens "when rain falls from the sky into a river or fount; all is water, for the rain that fell from heaven cannot be divided or separated from the water of the river."[32] John of the Cross boldly states that the individual at this stage "becomes God by participation."[33] These statements suggest that one no longer relates to God in prayer as an object outside oneself. God is realized in the seventh room as the deepest subject of one's experience, an indwelling presence inseparably identified with one's true spiritual self. God sees through one's eyes and loves through one's heart. The inner journey to the center of the soul leads to a return to the world in an abundant outpouring of creativity and service.

Implications for the Formation of Spiritual Directors

A brief presentation of Teresa's description of development in prayer is not intended to substitute for careful reading of her original works and other classic texts that have charted the journey of prayer. It is simply meant to kindle a desire for such further study. Teresa placed great value on study in the formation of confessors and spiritual directors. She wrote that "half-learned confessors have done my soul great harm and a truly learned man has never misguided me."[34] She learned through painful experience that poorly educated directors were more likely to impose on her their own misguided interpretations and unexamined assumptions about prayer. She understood that the study of theology and spirituality can expand a director's vision of the heights, depths and incredible variety of experiences that are possible in prayer. When this learning is grounded in experience directors are able to receive the unique prayer journeys of directees with greater understanding, discernment, and compassion.

Wise and well-educated directors are particularly needed at the key transitions that John of the Cross called the nights of sense and spirit. During these transitions surface manifestations of pervasive dissatisfaction, intellectual disorientation, inability to pray in the familiar ways, and emergence of previously unconscious feelings and desires can easily be mistaken for spiritual regression or psychological pathology. As directors we can fail to discern the graced emergence of contemplative prayer that is happening in the depths. A broad and deep vision of development in prayer can help us stay present to directees as they negotiate these difficult passages along the way to union with God.

For Further Reflection

1. What image or metaphor describes your personal spiritual journey?

2. Describe some benefits and cautions in using a "map" to describe authentic interior experiences as presented by Teresa of Ávila and John of the Cross.

3. Are you satisfied with your prayer life right now? If not, what do you find helpful?

4. What development have you noticed in your prayer over time? Has your relationship with God changed over time? Is there a relationship between the two?

Resources

Burrows, Ruth. *Fire Upon the Earth: Interior Castle Explored.* Denville, N.J.: Dimension Books, 1981.

The Collected Works of St. John of the Cross. Trans. Kieran Kavanaugh and Otilio Rodriguez. Washington, D.C.: ICS Publications, 1979.

Keating, Thomas. *Invitation to Love: The Way of Christian Contemplation*. Rockport, Mass.: Dimension Books, 1992.

May, Gerald. *The Dark Night of the Soul: A Psychiatrist Explores the Connection Between Darkness and Spiritual Growth*. San Francisco: HarperSanFrancisco, 2004.

Teresa of Ávila. *The Interior Castle*. Mahwah, N.J.: Paulist Press, 1979.

Listening to the Soul's Story
Psychology in Spiritual Direction Programs

In 1923, Sigmund Freud was writing to Pastor Oskar Pfister about the helpfulness of psychoanalysis in pastoral care.[35] In the years since then, spiritual direction and psychology have had an uneasy relationship. Like siblings, they have fought, contended for first place, merged, and dressed alike. In the century or so since psychology has been recognized as a discipline, spiritual directors have seen it as an enemy, an ally best kept at arm's length, a subordinate field, a welcome means of understanding and facilitating spiritual growth, or another vocabulary to describe the same terrain charted by the spiritual classics. After all, the root meaning of "psychology" is "soul story" and "psychotherapy" is "soul cure or healing."

Today many, if not most, spiritual formation programs assume that some understanding of psychology is essential to an informed and ethical practice of spiritual direction. My reflections here are based on my twenty-five years of experience as a spiritual director, twenty years of experience as a trainer of spiritual directors, and twelve years as a pastoral psychotherapist trained in self psychology.

Relationship between Spiritual Direction and Psychotherapy

I have come to believe that spiritual direction and psychotherapy are distinct but not separate processes. They lie along a continuum. At one end of this continuum is psychotherapy which focuses on the relief of painful psychic symptoms such as guilt, shame, anxiety, depression, and loneliness as well as destructive ways of organizing and interpreting the meaning of feelings and events. Yet psychotherapy also addresses the diffuse sense of emptiness and meaninglessness felt by so many in our society, a sense that is often seen as an indication of a loss of a sense of God and larger meaning. At the other end of the continuum, spiritual direction centers on the ways in which a person engages and relates to ultimate reality, ultimate value, or God. Yet the material for both processes, the directee's life experience, is the same: events, joys, disappointments, crises, feelings of being loved or abandoned, images, relationships, beliefs, movements that come in prayer — that is, all that is part of being human.[36]

Spiritual direction and psychotherapy, however, look at these same phenomena through different "lenses." Viewing an object through a telescope and then a microscope will yield very different yet equally valid aspects of the same thing and yield very different but equally valid understandings of it. Another analogy is to maps. An aeronautical map guides a pilot flying over a stretch of territory with different landmarks than a road map guides someone driving across the same terrain. Each guides in a way that is appropriate for that traveler's needs and journey.[37] Other helpful analogies are provided by John Veltri, SJ: a Venn diagram shows the areas where two different figures overlap and where they do not; a strand of the double helix of DNA has two different gene sequences intertwined yet distinct; a circle has different quadrants but each is an essential part of the whole.[38]

All psychology encompasses spirituality and all spirituality involves psychology.[39]

Spirituality and spiritual direction can enhance psychic growth just as psychotherapy can lead to spiritual growth. There are moments when spiritual direction is therapeutic and when therapy deals with spiritual questions. Someone who cannot feel loved by God as she struggles with the Principle and Foundation of the Spiritual Exercises of St. Ignatius might come to that sense after receiving empathic mirroring in therapy. Someone who has a profound experience in prayer of unity with self, humanity, and God might experience a level of self-cohesion unavailable in therapy. For me, the question is no longer "Is this direction or therapy?" but "At what end of the continuum are we spending most of our time?"

The theological framework undergirding a training program will influence the use it makes of psychology. Those who operate from the assumption that "God is not only the creator and sustainer of the universe but also an agent in a special way in particular events" will see psychology as more ancillary than those who see spirituality as "special sensitivity of some people to God's general action in the world."[40]

Integration of Psychology and Spirituality

What does all of this mean for training programs in spiritual direction? I think it implies that the psychological framework taught in a course should be integrated into a program's spiritual framework. Many programs use Jungian psychology as their psychological model. This implies that interns be encouraged to welcome recognition of the shadow and animus/anima and to minimize moral judgments on ways it might manifest itself. Since these are important steps in the individuation process, which is inherently spiritual, the welcoming back of split-off parts of the spiritual seeker is to be valued as a milestone on the road to actualization of the more archetypal realm of the self. Programs that emphasize a spirituality of self-discipline might integrate more easily with the Freudian metapsychology of biological drives, which must be reined in by the superego, and of narcissism, which must be supplanted by object love.

Another framework that is used in training programs is the transpersonal psychology of Ken Wilber.[41] It accords well with ecological and quantam-based spiritualities, and is a major source for Thomas Keating's psychology of Centering Prayer. Keating teaches that Centering Prayer helps persons to move beyond defensive "emotional programs for happiness" and find the True Self, "the Image of God in which every human being is created."[42] This concept of the True Self finds correspondences in object relations psychology.

Two neo-Freudian schools of psychology that are not commonly used as frameworks in training programs are object relations and self psychology. A body of literature that bridges object relations and spirituality exists, and a few writers have done the same for self psychology and spiritual direction.[43] These two schools give us a picture of how a person's spiritual core develops from birth and how it may have more influence over their lived spirituality than the ethical and moral teachings they are exposed to.[44] It is this spiritual core that is addressed in direction and which might need healing before a person can be open to God. These psychologies have broken out of the model of the discrete human self to the recognition that "we do not stop at our own skin," an insight taught in the world's spiritual traditions. This is an area which, in my view, has promise but needs development.

Whatever framework is used, programs have found it helpful to address several psychological topics in the course of their formation of spiritual directors. Let's now look briefly at some of those topics.

Personality Theory

Most programs teach the Enneagram and the Myers-Briggs Type Indicator. These are relatively easy to grasp without a lot of psychoanalytic background, and are useful modes of understanding directees. In addition, each has a substantial literature relating the theory to prayer, spirituality, and spiritual growth. The Myers-Briggs system is rooted in Jungian psychology and fleshes out Jung's theories on individuation.[45] It is also the more empirically based of the two. The Enneagram's origins are less clear, but it is certainly influenced by Eastern spirituality.[46] Its teaching that each person has an essence, a "word that God spoke" when each was created, accords with some psychoanalytic theories that speak of a core self or a nuclear program of the self that must be realized if the person is to attain authentic maturity.

The relative accessibility of these two typologies can be a problem if the program teaches them in a cursory way. Weekend workshops or short lectures do not do justice to the subject. Interns can apply this categorizing to others and to themselves in an insensitive and unnuanced way. Ideally interns are given instruction into these personality theories gradually, over a period of at least several months, and are encouraged to look at the experienced reality, first of themselves, then of other people before proceeding to interpret all their behavior in reference to the type. Related to this is the issue of stereotyping. I have seen interns who would never dream of engaging in racial or ethnic stereotyping make sweeping judgments of others based on what they think is their Enneagram type.

Developmental Psychology

There is general consensus that developmental psychology is an important part of the psychological component of a training program. Along with self-understanding for trainees, developmental theory, such as that of Erik Erikson or Robert Kegan,[47] provides a helpful hermeneutic for intern directors as they seek to be spiritual companions. It sharpens their sense of what images of God are likely to resonate with a particular person, how developed their moral sense is likely to be, what kind of prayer is possible. It also sharpens the director's discernment of the directee's capacity to "go inside" to notice feelings, images, realizations, and movements that lead to greater openness to God's call in prayer and in daily life.[48] A knowledge of developmental psychology should lead us as directors to become more empathic companions, less frustrated with directees who do not "cooperate," less likely to blame either ourselves or the directee when direction does not proceed as expected, and less likely to demand from directees what they are not capable of.

My experience of teaching the developmental theory of Robert Kegan has been very positive. Based on the work of Jean Piaget and D. W. Winnecott, among others, Kegan's articulation of the evolution of the self harmonizes with Lonergan's theology of self-transcendence as well as with Fowler's ideas on faith development.

Kegan's wise and compassionate writings stress the need for confirmation as well as challenge for us all wherever we are along the road of life. His metaphor of the "culture of embeddedness" gives intern directors a fine image for a way they might serve directees. Of course, heedfulness about jumping to conclusions without a thorough knowledge of a person are always in order as are cautions against a hierarchical "maturity morality."

Diagnostic Considerations

As spiritual directors, we do not need an extensive understanding of psychopathology, but we do need a general awareness of psychological disorders that can help us to discern when a referral to a therapist, psychologist, or psychiatrist is advisable. In my opinion a presentation on the subject in a workshop format with case studies is helpful to trainees. Gerald May's *Care of Mind/Care of Spirit* has a useful chapter on psychiatric concerns (post-traumatic stress disorder is not included) that would make a good resource for directors, even though it is based on the superseded *Diagnostic and Statistical Manual III* of the American Psychological Association.[49]

As Heinz Kohut discovered, today's industrialized societies have more people suffering from a narcissistic sense of emptiness than people experiencing conflicts between biological drives and superego constraints. Many come to spiritual direction in the hope of finding a sense of purpose and peace. Thus, some knowledge of personality or character disorders, imparted through a workshop as above, will be useful since we are more likely to encounter persons burdened with them than with psychosis. Of course, these disorders of the self are very often accompanied by substance abuse, mood disorders, and other psychiatric disorders described by May. To an extent, these conditions are shared by all humans, and they are less sharply delineated than psychiatric ones, but a general knowledge of character disorders will alert us to the fact that a referral to a therapist might be in order so that the directee can benefit more fully from direction.

None of this is to suggest that current directors or trainees should be encouraged to disengage from directees when they refer them to mental health professionals. Saying, in effect, "Go to therapy to get fixed up; then come back and we can talk about God," promotes a split view of the human person. In most cases, direction and therapy enhance each other.

Having advised some general education on diagnosis, I hasten to add that the diagnostic or medical lens is not the one most fruitfully used by the spiritual director. Since the lens determines what the viewer sees, it will show sickness rather than the ways in which human being's desire for the "more than" or God gets sidetracked or appears in unusual forms.

Other Psychological Considerations

Spiritual directors in training should develop the capacity to discern the extent to which a directee's spirituality is functioning to promote stability, cohesion, and structure as well as how much challenge to critically examine that spirituality the directee can withstand without fragmenting psychologically. Also, they need to be aware of a directee's using spiritual direction as therapy by staying at the psychic pain or symptomatic end of the continuum or by acting out transferential issues with the director. Vigilance is also required when using an approach that integrates spirituality and psychology, in order to avoid collapsing spiritual direction into therapy and thereby losing its distinctive character and purpose.

Transference and countertransference are phenomena that should be in the awareness of a potential spiritual director. Such information serves to normalize these processes and provides guidelines for ethical conduct on the part of the intern director. It also imparts a firmer sense of when either transference or countertransference has reached a point when referral to a therapist or to another director is advisable.[50]

Presentations on spiritual direction with selected populations can be helpful to interns. Topics might be direction with trauma and abuse survivors, with persons dealing with substance abuse and recovery, with lesbian and gay people, with the sick and dying. My colleagues and I present most of the topics mentioned above in a series of workshops that have didactic input as well as personal and group processing of the material.

Listening Skills

Most programs consider the development of listening skills essential to the preparation of spiritual directors. This is usually addressed through handouts and role-play and is commonly done in the first ten or so meetings of staff-led supervision groups. The handouts are often created by the supervision staff and cover basic skills such as attending, following, paraphrasing feeling and content, and challenging. Trainees work in pairs with the supervisor "floating" among them or in a small group. A more structured approach to listening which is occasionally used is found in Gerard Egan's *The Skilled Helper.*[51]

Work with the Unconscious

Religious traditions around the world have a rich legacy of writings and experience of God speaking through visions and dreams. The Christian mystical tradition has emphasized communication with the God within. Since Freud's "discovery" of the unconscious, it has been seen as a privileged place of divine encounter. Dream work and active imagination are ways to access a mode of knowing ourselves and the ways we are being called that go beyond our personal and societal defenses. Ideally they will be presented as means to access the stirrings of the Spirit in our communities and our world as well as individual intrapsychic wisdom. Since Jungian dream work is accompanied by a great deal of literature on dreams and spirituality and dreams and the individuation process, it is most commonly used. Other types of dream work such as existential or Gestalt may also be useful.[52] Interns should develop an awareness of which directees are likely to become disorganized by imaginative processes and the dangers of using them as an escape from life and prayer.

Psychology in the Supervision Process

Supervision is probably the single most important element in the process of internalizing the values of a program and appropriating the identity of spiritual director. The modeling of integrating and differentiating psychology and spiritual direction experienced in supervision is the model which most interns will take away with them. Barry and Connolly state that the purpose of supervision is the development of spiritual directors as "persons whose hearts are open and discerning, whose faith, hope, and love are almost tangible."[53] For this reason they counsel that supervision focus on the countertransference of the director, not on the dynamics of the directee.

This is wise advice. It promotes the intern director's growth as a person who is more able to be present to a directee and more able to use her countertransference as a connection point rather than an obstacle in the relationship. Countertransference, by definition, has psychological dimensions and points to ways in which the intern director needs psychological as well as spiritual healing. In this situation, countertransference means the unconscious response of the intern director to the directee. This response can be based on past relationships, personal biases, needs, and other projections. This probably can be handled best by the supervisor musing with the intern about the wounded, unfinished place in him or her. Then the intern can address the issue elsewhere — through personal work, spiritual direction, or therapy.

There are times, however, when discussion of the dynamics of the directee is appropriate: when the directee needs to be referred, when the directee is in danger harming self or others, when the intern is responding to the directee in a way that is not helpful.

Transformative Effects of Psychology in Spiritual Direction Programs

Spiritual direction interns find that exposure to psychology is a great help in self-knowledge, an important element in their own spiritual growth. This also makes them more sensitive to places in themselves that are apt to become tangled in countertransference as well as to other areas of unfreedom that impede their ability to give themselves fully to this ministry. This exposure also helps them to name many things that they know intuitively and act upon unconsciously and to understand their intuition in the light of a larger context. Thus, spiritual direction interns tend to gain both more confidence in their own psychological sense of people and a clearer sense of the limits of their psychological knowledge.

Participants often find themselves listening to those closest to them with "new ears" and understanding them at deeper levels and report that their personal as well as ministerial life is enriched. Work with the unconscious also helps trainees to trust the guidance that comes from that source and to marvel at the way that God works in and through them.

Psychology and spirituality both engage the human spirit but for distinct, not dichotomous, purposes. The boundary between them is fluid and, in many instances, those who walk in the uncharted territory they share must do so with little tradition to draw on and no adequate language to describe what they see and hear and feel. I have put forward some ideas about the psychological components and facets in formation programs with the time and resources to carry them out. Even more important is sharing with intern directors an attitude that is open to the workings of the Spirit in the human heart.

 For Further Reflection

1. How do you see the relationship between spiritual direction and psychology? Have you experienced moments in spiritual direction that were therapeutic? What was the result?

2. Do you tend to understand God's action as happening directly in your life or more as mediated through the laws of nature, other people, happenings in the world? How does that belief influence your view of the use of psychology in spiritual direction?

3. What is your experience with personality typologies? How have they helped you to understand others? How have they gotten in the way of understanding others?

4. What would be your criteria for referring a directee for psychological help?

Resources

Barnes, Ronald, SJ. "Psychology and Spirituality: Meeting at the Boundaries." *The Way Supplement* 69 (Autumn 1990): 29–42.

Barry, William A., and William J. Connolly. *The Practice of Spiritual Direction.* San Francisco: HarperSanFrancisco, 1982.

Bulkeley, Kelly. *The Wilderness of Dreams: Exploring the Religious Meaning of Dreams in Modern Western Culture.* Albany: State University of New York Press, 1994.

Conn, Walter E. *The Desiring Self: Rooting Pastoral Counseling and Spiritual Direction in Self-Transcendence.* Mahwah, N.J.: Paulist Press, 1998.

Egan, Gerard. *The Skilled Helper: A Problem-Management and Opportunity-Development Approach to Helping.* Stamford, Conn.: Wadsworth Publishing, 2004.

Empereur, James. *The Enneagram and Spiritual Direction: Nine Paths to Spiritual Guidance.* New York: Continuum, 1997.

Erikson, Erik. *Childhood and Society.* New York: W. W. Norton & Company, 1950, 1993.

Gillespie, C. Kevin. "Listening for Grace: Self Psychology and Spiritual Direction." In *Handbook of Spirituality for Ministers,* vol. 1, ed. Robert Wicks, 347–61. Mahwah, N.J.: Paulist Press, 1995.

Grant, Brian. *A Theology for Pastoral Psychotherapy: God's Play in Sacred Spaces.* New York: Haworth Press, 2001.

Grant, W. Harold, Mary Magdala Thompson, and Thomas E. Clarke. *From Image to Likeness: A Jungian Path in the Gospel Journey.* Mahwah, N.J.: Paulist Press, 1983.

Helminiak, Daniel A. *Spiritual Development: an Interdisciplinary Study.* Chicago: Loyola University Press, 1987.

Johnson, Robert. *Inner Work: Using Dreams and Active Imagination for Personal Growth.* San Francisco: HarperSanFrancisco, 1986.

Keating, Thomas. *Invitation to Love: The Way of Christian Contemplation.* New York: Continuum, 2000.

Kegan, Robert. *The Evolving Self: Problems and Process in Human Development.* Cambridge: Harvard University Press, 1982.

Liebert, Elizabeth. *Changing Life Patterns: Adult Development in Spiritual Direction.* 2nd ed. Atlanta: Chalice Press, 2001.

Malone, Janet, CND. "The Helping Relationships." *Human Development* 21, no. 4 (Winter 2000): 5–13.

May, Gerald. *Care of Mind, Care of Spirit: Psychiatric Dimensions of Spiritual Direction.* San Francisco: HarperSanFrancisco, 1982.

Meng, Heinrich, and Ernst L. Freud, eds. *Psychoanalysis and Faith: The Letters of Sigmund Freud and Oskar Pfister.* New York: Basic Books, 1963.

Mueller, Craig. "Dreams and Spiritual Direction." *Presence* 4, no. 3 (September 1998): 15–23.

Murphy, Nancey. "Nonreductive Physicalism: Philosophical Issues." In *Whatever Happened to the Soul? Scientific and Theological Portraits of Human Nature,* ed. Warren S. Brown, Nancey Murphy, H. Newton Malony, 127–48. Theology and the Sciences. Minneapolis: Fortress Press, 1998.

Schermer, Victor. *Spirit and Psyche: A New Paradigm for Psychology, Psychoanalysis, and Psychotherapy.* London: Jessica Kingsley Publishers, 2003.

Taylor, Jeremy. *Where People Fly and Water Runs Uphill: Using Dreams to Tap the Power of the Unconscious.* New York: Warner Books, 1992.

Veltri, John, SJ. "For Those Who Accompany Others on Their Inward Journey." In *Orientations* 2, part B. Guelph, Ontario: Loyola Press, 1979, 513–72. See *www.sentex.net/~jveltri/guide/spirit.html.*

Whitehead, Evelyn Eaton, and James D. Whitehead. *Christian Life Patterns: The Psychological Challenges and Religious Invitations of Adult Life.* New ed. New York: Crossroad, 1992.

Wilber, Ken. *Integral Psychology: Consciousness, Spirit, Psychology, Therapy.* Boston: Shambhala Publications, 2000.

———. *No Boundary: Eastern and Western Approaches to Personal Growth.* Boston: Shambhala Publications, 1979.

Maturing in Faith
Stages in the Adult Spiritual Journey

With the exception of Ignatius of Loyola's *Spiritual Exercises,* the two most influential paradigms in my formation as a spiritual director have been the development theory of James W. Fowler and the theory of individuation espoused by Carl G. Jung. Fowler and Jung offer critical lenses that assist us as directors in listening to and discerning the spiritual experience of adults.

Within the history of Christianity, almost all authors of its spiritual classics portray a progressive movement in describing the lifelong journey toward union with God. Two such maps in the history of mystical theology are offered by Bonaventure, a thirteenth-century Franciscan, and by John of the Cross, a sixteenth-century Carmelite. Bonaventure is responsible for portraying this path with the classical descriptors of the purgative, illuminative, and unitive stages in the spiritual quest. John of the Cross describes the journey as passing through four phases — the dark night of the senses, illumination, the dark night of the spirit, and rebirth.[54]

As life-giving as the work of Bonaventure and John of the Cross is, they wrote for a culture where their language spoke more directly to the contemporary level of human consciousness of its day. Our culture today, in the twenty-first century, is quite different. James Fowler and Carl Jung offer a language and categories, similar to Bonaventure and John, to describe this journey in a way, that for many people is more relevant to twenty-first century culture, espe-cially in the West. Exploring the spiritual path Fowler and Jung map for the human soul helps us to recover the treasure of our spiritual classics, making them more accessible and relevant to us.

Fowler[55] offers four stages that map the terrain in our faith journey as adults. These stages point to ways of structuring ultimate value and meaning in our lives. They are sequential and the transitions from one to the other can be quite painful, involving the loss of meaning and the death of our operating image of God. Jung's individuation process[56] also involves four phases which, in my experience, complement those of Fowler. While Fowler tends to be more cognitive and deals with the conscious, Jung emphasizes the affective and unconscious.

Adults tend to seek spiritual direction when their way of structuring ultimate reality and meaning in life unravels. Let's look at each of these stages and consider how we as spiritual directors might minister to someone in transition from one stage to another.

Stage 1 / Ultimate Reality and Meaning Defined by External Culture

Fowler describes this first stage as "conventional" and "tacit." While conventional means conforming to external standards, tacit implies a lack of conscious reflection on our lived experience.[57] Jung uses the term "persona" to refer to the face we choose to show to the outside world.[58] "Who I am" is primarily determined by the values of our family, peers, and culture. We have a built-in resistance to asking the question "Who am I?" It usually takes a dramatic event (e.g., a profound religious experience or some trauma) to propel us out of this mode into a deeper awareness of self. Often as spiritual directors, we will help the individual verbalize, explore, and expand this experience, which could well be a directee's first recognized experience of the living God.

Stage 2 / Self-Defined World of Ultimate Meaning and Reality

Transition to this stage is not automatic, and some of us may seek to elude it. However, if we negotiate this transition successfully, we begin to see emerge a new construct and understanding for ultimate meaning and reality. Fowler refers to this stage as "individuated reflective" dominated by an "executive ego,"[59] while for Jung it centers on the conscious ego.[60] At this stage, we operate out of an explicitly conscious self-defined ideology that strongly influences our lifestyle and determines our choice of intentional community. Many of the "isms" (e.g. environmentalism, feminism) receive their momentum and passion from the faith commitment of people at this stage. Once we are solidified at this stage, we feel quite secure, comfortable, and sufficient. We draw on support from a community of like-minded people and are often intolerant of those who do not share our values and worldview. At the peak of this stage, we may not feel a need for spiritual direction. However, when our ideological construct of reality begins to crack with inconsistencies, and the structures that energized our lives begin to lose their authority and power, we may seek spiritual direction.

Stage 3 / Ultimate Meaning and Value in Denied or Repressed Experience

At this point, often around midlife, we begin to discern limits within our previous ideological construct. This new awareness may compel an encounter with aspects of the unconscious — that against which we have been defending ourselves for the first half of life. Beginning to sense the limits of the rational, we are drawn to pay attention to memories, dreams, and feelings that begin to engage our consciousness. Fowler calls this stage "conjunctive" faith.[61] It incorporates the rational and nonrational, the present and the past, symbol and ideology. In Jung's individuation process, this activity is identified as embracing our "shadow" — that part of ourselves we have spent much energy repressing.[62]

As spiritual directors, we may also explore this third stage through the lens of shame — which should be distinguished from guilt.[63] Shame refers to nonrational negative judgmental feelings strongly affecting how we feel about ourselves. Guilt pertains to something objectively wrong that we have done. Although sometimes shame and guilt might coincide with some lived experience, shame is the gnawing feeling that deep within there is something flawed, which if allowed to come to light would threaten our identity and security. There is a lurking belief that "if those who respect me really knew me, they would not think as highly of me as they do." A directee would have difficulty objectively defending this position, but in the experience of shame, the nonrational towers over the rational, and much energy has been expended in compensating for this phenomenon.

At this point in spiritual direction, we can assist a directee to befriend and incorporate into consciousness the energy previously employed repressing his or her shadow or shame. In addition, the directee becomes free to resurrect behaviors and values from childhood or adolescence (e.g., religious devotions, community customs) as well as discern positive elements in worldviews other than his or her own (e.g., other religious traditions).

Stage 4 / Ultimate Meaning and Value in God's One Sustaining Act of Creation

At some point, we might discover that the darkness embraced at the previous stage begins to yield to a more external mystical awareness of God's presence in creation, history, and our personal experience of life. Fowler classifies this stage as "universalizing faith" and participating in the "commonwealth of being."[64] Jung viewed this phase as the culmination of the individuation process — living out of one's true self.[65]

Another way of exploring this stage is through an insight of John Macmurray, a twentieth-century Scottish philosopher. He writes about "the one creative act of God" and the invitation individuals have to align their conscious selves with this act.[66] At this stage of development, directees are often aware that their lives are receiving momentum and direction from "another." Janet Ruffing describes this experience as "mutuality with God — a feature of mature spiritual life."[67] "I am where God is," and "God breathes me," phrases attributed to Rumi, a thirteenth-century Persian mystic, may also help to explore this new consciousness.

It is important to realize that at this point of the spiritual journey we have reached, and are invited to live out of, our True Self — the God within, which is the goal of Jung's individuation process. Thus the God within merges with the God present in creation and history. Ignatius of Loyola's "finding God in all things" offers another way of viewing this mystical state.

Implications for Spiritual Direction

William Barry and William Connolly define spiritual direction "as help given to another which enables that person to pay attention to God's personal communication to him or her, to respond to this personally communicating God, to grow in intimacy with this God, and to live out the consequences of the relationship."[68] This is especially true during the dry periods of transition from one stage to another. The assumption is that God is in communication with the directee and that the relationship provides a container to explore just how God is present during a period of darkness and aridity. It may even be the case that, during a period of transition, the relationship with a director might be the primary support and motivation to persevere.

Transition from one stage to another is not inevitable. It involves a transformation of both cognitive and affective structures and can take a considerable period of time. Remaining faithful to a life of prayer during this time is critical. The faith of a directee may be sustained and nourished primarily by our faith that God is present and acting. It is most desirable that we have lived the journey we are facilitating. Although supervision is normative for our spiritual direction ministry, it is especially critical when we cannot identify with the pattern (as distinct from content) a directee is verbalizing. Also, if there is an obvious lack of progress, we might do well to suggest that a directee work with a therapist, while at the same time continuing the spiritual direction relationship.

With each stage, the scope of religious experience broadens and the method of prayer that will lead a directee into a new stage changes. Our role as directors is to listen for a different mode of God's initiative in the life of a directee. It is also important to notice how practicing a certain form of prayer influences the quality of the directee's daily life. Those in Stage 2 (ideology formulated through ego consciousness) tend to identify religious experience with their ideological commitment and desires, and thus their preferred prayer might tend more toward *lectio divina* or meditation. Those in Stage 3 (confrontation with the unconscious) might find Centering Prayer, active imagination, or communicating with God about a dream interpretation more nourishing than more traditional methods. Here it is important that we be open to the many possible manifestations of God's initiative. Mystical union usually marks Stage 4 (unitive faith), which an individual may celebrate through the prayer of quiet or passive contemplation. However, this does not mean that, at times, past forms of prayer might not also be helpful.

Finally, we should realize that many more individuals in our culture are being invited to a spiritual life at the higher stages. Some view this as either an evolution or revolution of consciousness that humanity in the Western world is experiencing. As spiritual directors, we should respect the many signs of this phenomenon (e.g. New Age culture, therapeutic culture) and be convinced of the great value our ministry of spiritual direction has to respond to this thirst.

✤ For Further Reflection

1. Why might it be important to have a model of adult spiritual development that is appropriate to our changing times?

2. How might you recognize a directee who is living is Stage 2 of adult spiritual development? What type of life experiences might be presented?

3. Have you ever demanded or required that someone act or think in a way that was beyond their level of spiritual development? Give concrete examples from directees, if possible.

4. As a director, how can you be present to how your own transitions influence the quality of your listening and presence?

✿ Resources

Conn, Walter. *Christian Conversion: A Developmental Interpretation of Autonomy and Surrender.* Mahwah, N.J.: Paulist Press, 1986.

Finley, James. *Christian Meditation: Experiencing the Presence of God.* San Francisco: HarperCollins, 2004.

Fowler, James W. *Becoming Adult, Becoming Christian: Adult Development and Christian Faith.* Rev. ed. San Francisco: Jossey-Bass Publishers, 2000.

Keating, Thomas. *Invitation to Love: The Way of Christian Contemplation.* New York: Continuum, 2002.

Kegan, Robert. *The Evolving Self: Problem and Process in Human Development.* Cambridge, Mass.: Harvard University Press, 1982.

Liebert, Elizabeth. *Changing Life Patterns.* Mahwah, N.J.: Paulist Press, 1992.

May, Gerald G. *The Dark Night of the Soul.* San Francisco: HarperSanFrancisco, 2004.

Moore, Robert L., ed. *Carl Jung and Christian Spirituality.* Mahwah, N.J.: Paulist Press, 1988.

———. *Facing the Dragon: Confronting Personal and Spiritual Grandiosity.* Wilmette, Ill.: Chiron Publications, 2003.

Morrison, Andrew P. *The Culture of Shame.* New York: Ballantine Books, 1996.

Parks, Sharon. *The Critical Years: The Young Adult Search for a Faith to Live By.* San Francisco: HarperSanFrancisco, 1986.

Reiser, William. *Seeking God in All Things: Theology and Spiritual Direction.* Collegeville, Minn.: Liturgical Press, 2004.

Stein, Murray. *Transformation: Emergence of the Self.* College Station: Texas A&M University Press, 1998.

Storr, Anthony. *The Essential Jung.* Princeton, N.J.: Princeton University Press, 1981.

Ulanov, Ann Belford. *Religion and the Spiritual in Carl Jung.* Mahwah, N.J.: Paulist Press, 1999.

Timmerman, Joan H. *Sexuality and Spiritual Growth.* New York: Crossroad, 1992.

Embracing the Wisdom of the Body
Feelings and Spiritual Direction

Several years ago while in Lithuania I had the opportunity to purchase a piece of whimsical black pottery — a canister jar with a lid. A figure sits on top of the canister and a cityscape is painted below. Upon showing it to some Lithuanian friends, I was told that it was based on a Lithuanian fairy tale. The story begins as many good tales often do, once upon a time. "Once upon a time a couple had their first child. He was perfect in all the important ways, but he did have a strange hump on his back. His parents in their desire to love him and spare him from any embarrassment removed all the mirrors from their house. His mother made all his clothes and saw that his hump was artfully disguised. At home, no one ever referred to the unusual hump he had on his back. He grew up doing all the things young children do. He was mostly happy, but he did realize that he was a little bit different than his friends. Sometimes he was teased about the hump on his back, but he had never really seen it himself. One day when he was out walking in the forest he came upon a clear pool of water. The water was deep and dark, and he could clearly see his own reflection. For the first time he could see his hump. Being quite a brave boy, he decided to remove his shirt and look at himself carefully. He removed his shirt and looked deeply into the pool at his reflection. Much to his own surprise and delight, he discovered this strange hump on his back was a pair of marvelous wings! Being a very ordinary boy in most ways, he did the most natural thing he could think of — he began to fly over the city where he lived!"

I loved the story, and it made my pottery piece even more special. Mostly I loved the realization that we all carry "humps" around with us in life. Often we realize they are a part of our reality, and even if I and others ignore their presence the moment comes when we must be brave and look clearly at our own reflection. When we do that, the very activity of being that real with ourselves helps us to fly.

The story provides me a wonderful metaphor for spiritual direction. A spiritual direction session is a time when directees look bravely and clearly at themselves, and we have the opportunity to witness the brave and gracious activity in which they are involved. This tale illustrates for me the manner in which our body carries the wisdom that we need for growth. When we listen reverently to the stories of our life, we cannot help but notice what it is that encumbers us and needs to be looked at so that we might fly. Our bodies are a munificent gift from God and a treasure chest of information about the ways we can grow.

Wisdom of the Body Tools

How then as spiritual directors can we be with another and use the wisdom of the body to support the spiritual journey? What tools should we teach our students as they prepare for the ministry of spiritual direction? I'd like to share with you two concepts that assist me in spiritual direction conversations. The first draws upon the Enneagram system and invites us to notice whether my instinctual response to reality comes first from the head, the heart, or the gut. The second is based upon my belief that naming feelings is only an initial step in accessing body wisdom. After naming our feelings, we must feel our feelings, reverence our feelings, and then allow the feelings to be our teachers and guides. In addition, I suggest that our directees need not have knowledge of these tools in order for us to use them effectively in the spiritual direction relationship.

Integrating Head, Heart, and Gut

The Enneagram[69] system describes three types of people. These are frequently described as head, heart, or gut people. Those who lead from the head approach life first from their thinking function, those who lead from the heart look first to relationships, and those who lead from the gut approach life from their feeling function. In similar circumstances, for example, how to make a decision concerning an invitation, different individuals will have different initial reactions. A head person would probably consult their monthly planner to see if the date is clear and then would consider the logistics of getting to and from the event. A heart person first allows how delightful it would be to attend the event and might wonder who else received an invitation. The gut person has a quick feeling response without much practical consideration to whether or not he or she wishes to go to the event. Each of these responses is valid and begins to inform our choices. What we realize as we mature in life is that we need to look not just at our first reaction. We make valid decisions when we take all of these reactions into consideration. So we all need to consult our monthly planner and make sure that we are able to attend the event. We listen to our enthusiasm about going and wonder who else will be there. We notice our own desires about being part of this gathering. As we consider all of this information, we can come to a well-informed choice and decision.

This example illustrates simply that we each have a head, a heart, and a gut. The most integrated moments in our life are when we allow the head, the heart, and the gut to speak to one another. As we listen to the harmony in these three voices and stand erect in our current reality, we have a wondrous ability to move confidently in the world. It is from this place that we are able to make well-grounded and informed decisions and be our best self.

It is our body that carries the head, the heart, and the gut. The body is the instrument we have for hearing the harmony we so greatly desire in our relationships with ourselves, others, creation, and God. As we reverently attend to our thinking, our relating, and our feelings, and give them the opportunity to communicate with one another, we come to moments of integration, to experiences of grace. As I listen to the "stories" in another's life, I can sometimes hear whether he or she is leading from the head, the heart, or the gut. The head person might describe all the circumstances of the experience, will nuance the story with details and information and will often have difficulty making the final decision toward movement. A heart person I had in spiritual direction once told me that she needed to unroll the entire script, complete with characters and scenery, before she could begin to look at her own place in the story. Gut people often begin with a short initial story or event, and then will share and feel feelings that, sometimes difficult in their breadth or depth, relate to the initial story. These are wonderful moments to invite directee to move more deeply into the story by moving more deeply into the wisdom of the body.

When the head person finishes giving me the details of a story, I can gently inquire about how this decision affects the relationships in his or her life. I might invite the directee to notice what happens interiorly as these experiences are shared. I notice that it is seldom helpful to ask head people how they feel about a particular experience. Access to the feeling place more often comes by inviting people to notice interior responses to what is being shared. While the question is ultimately addressing the same concern, the access through noticing is generally much easier for a head person than using a "what are you feeling" question. Noticing what happens interiorly seems to keep the attention focused in the thinking function, and my desire is to notice more of the body's wisdom through accessing the relating and feeling function. I recall a directee who once was sharing a difficult experience. She was able to say to me, "I get a pain in my stomach when I talk about this." Using those words as an invitation to look more carefully at her interior response, I asked if she had an image to describe that pain in her stomach. She said, "It's like a growling dog with chomping teeth." As I invited her to notice what this growling dog needed from her she delightfully replied, "A good brushing and some other dogs with which to play." As we talked, she could make the connection that she needed other people to care about what was happening. She also needed to be attentive to her feeling responses to what was occurring in her own life related to this situation. Accessing this wisdom through her bodily response to the experience and working with the feelings through the image provided a rich source of information.

Heart people often have wondrous stories to share with me in direction. I must be careful not to get caught in the details or in trying to understand all the characters. Imagining the initial story as a backdrop for the deeper story that the directee needs to share helps me to stay focused. Heart people are well aware of how others are and will be affected by the choices they are making. What is more important for them to attend to is how they themselves will be affected by the choices being made. "Tell me a little more about how you are feeling" or "What do you want to do?" are often challenging and enlightening invitations for someone in this space. It is also helpful to listen carefully for information that grounds the experience being shared.

A gut person will often name the feelings that accompany the experiences being shared and frequently will be connected to the affect of the feelings being shared. While the grace of having a safe place in which to share feelings is invaluable to a person in this space he or she also needs to gently consider others. I recently sat with a directee who had experienced the loss of a parent. She lived at a distance from the rest of her family and, after the initial experience of the wake and funeral, returned to her own family and job. When she went back into her parent's home about two months later, she was amazed at the ease with which her siblings who lived nearby could walk into the family home when this was still so difficult for her. The absence of her father was still a raw wound in her life. Those siblings who lived nearby had returned to the family home many times and that shock of initial absence was less harsh for them. My directee, however, still became teary each time she opened the hall closet and noticed her dad's coats were no longer hanging there. She felt isolated in the depth of her feelings. After her visit to the family home, she began to draft a letter to her siblings telling them she was feeling rushed and ignored in her grieving process. We spent some time being gentle and caring toward her grief, and then began to talk about the letter she was writing to her siblings. As she began to speak about this, I found myself saying, "Remember, they are hurting also." The words had a profound effect on her. As she sat in the silence that these simple words created in her interior, I could almost see her visibly soften. After a few minutes she said to me, "I still need to write this letter, but it will be different now." As her relating, or "heart" function came into relationship with her feeling "gut" and thinking "head" function she discovered a more integrated way of responding to this situation.

These simple stories illustrate how we as directors can help a person to access the wisdom of the body. Tools like the Enneagram can be used in an integrated fashion within a direction session without us ever needing to teach the tool to the directee.

Moving from Naming Feelings to Gaining Wisdom

When using the feeling function during a direction session, I believe it is critical to realize that it is not sufficient simply to "name" our feelings. When we name feelings, we are still operating from the thinking function. We begin to relate to our feelings when we *feel* them. For example, I can name sadness as a feeling connected with the death of someone I love and still protect myself from my own feeling of sadness. I begin to integrate feelings into a rightful place in my life when I allow myself to feel my feelings. But this is only an initial step. We must delve more deeply into our feelings for them to help us to live our lives as more whole and holier people.

Our bodies carry the feelings that are associated with every moment of our lives and are rich resources to us in our life journey. However, we frequently learn to ignore or suppress our feelings as if we could forget them or separate them from the tapestry of our lives. I know how to try, sometimes with apparent success, to forget feelings. I know how to suppress feelings. I know how to talk myself out of feelings. My experience tells me that each of those attempts, while at times moderately successful, ultimately fails. When the same wound is tapped again, I respond with more emotion that is actually appropriate for the event. Something different needs to happen in my body and in the way I respect my feeling responses if I want to allow my body to reveal its wisdom.

We often read in books on spiritual direction about the importance of feelings. John of the Cross writes passionate poetry about his feeling relationship with God. Ignatius of Loyola tells us we must have a felt knowledge of God. Psychological theory reminds us of the need to integrate feelings appropriate with the experiences of life in order to be well balanced. As spiritual directors, many of us recognize the need to be attentive to the feelings of the directee within the context of the spiritual direction conversation. In spiritual direction conversations, we invite people to name the feelings associated with the relationships or situation that are being shared with us. As I said above, I've come to believe that naming feelings is only the first step. I believe that we need to be involved in these four movements:

1. Name the feelings

2. Feel the feelings

3. Reverence/care for the feelings

4. Allow the feelings to be our teacher and a place of wisdom.

Frequently when I sit with someone in spiritual direction, I become aware of moments when he or she trips over feelings. While telling me about what is happening in any arena of life, the feelings associated with a particular event or set of circumstances become apparent. This is often found in the body expression, in the choice of words, or in the silence that comes as the directee shares from his or her deepest places. These are wondrous moments in our time together. If I can use these opportunities to gently invite the directee to name what he or she is feeling, and then to notice how the body holds these feelings, we can move to what is most important, reverencing the feelings.

In reverencing feelings, the focusing process becomes most critical.[70] Here we gently remind and reassure our directees with words like these: "Do not try to change your feelings," "Do not try to figure them out," "Do not ask them any questions." Instead we invite a simple acknowledgement of the feeling presence and a caring acceptance of them. What a gift. Can you remember moments when you were cared for in this way and the incredible healing that comes through that experience? For me, this reverencing reflects the grace-filled way in which God loves me at every moment of my life. Almost always, when I care for a feeling without any need, desire, or push to change it, the feeling itself moves or reveals a deeper reality. This is when feelings become my teacher. They remind me of events from my past history and give me a clue why I feel so strongly in this moment about a situation. They give me access to the child within who needs healing and hearing. They connect me to the larger world and allow me to see with new perspective. They are relieved at being given space and air and a right to be. They take their rightful place inside of me and come into proper proportion with all the circumstances of my life. When this happens with a directee, these moments are the most powerful, most grace-filled, and most reverent times in my work of spiritual direction.

Using the Tools

As in the examples using Enneagram theory, I do not need to teach the focusing process to directees in order to integrate it into direction sessions. What I do need with both of these tools is a secure knowledge of the wisdom they contain and personal experience with the process. I believe the best teacher is my own spiritual director, who integrates these tools into her work with me in direction. That means at times I will seek out a director who is well informed with these processes and will ask her to use them within her direction conversation with me. This is particularly helpful when I am first learning the process. As we teach these tools to the people in our formation programs, we provide them with concrete, practical ways of helping directees access the wisdom contained in their bodies.

For Further Reflection

1. How do you see the relationship between spiritual direction and the body?

2. How might your type (head, heart, or gut) get in the way of helping another to pay attention to the wisdom of the body?

3. What feelings might be challenging for you to help another to explore and honor?

4. What might help you to be a more "embodied" listener? Give specific examples of acknowledging your body in life, prayer, and spiritual direction.

 Resources

Campbell, Peter A. and Edwin M. McMahon. *Bio-Spirituality: Focusing as a Way to Grow.* Chicago: Loyola University Press, 1985.

Empereur, James. *The Enneagram and Spiritual Direction: Nine Paths to Spiritual Guidance.* New York: Continuum, 2001.

Zuercher, Suzanne, OSB. *Enneagram Companions: Growing in Relationships and Spiritual Direction.* Notre Dame, Ind.: Ave Maria Press, 2000.

Tending the Sacred Fire
Sexuality and Spiritual Direction

"The sexual and spiritual parts of the human personality," Scott Peck said, "lie so close together that we cannot arouse one without arousing the other." As the words penetrated, I sat up straighter in my chair, body and mind suddenly alert. A neophyte spiritual director in the early 1990s, I had come to a public lecture to hear Dr. Peck. This statement came in response to a question I no longer remember, but the words shimmered in me evoking the combination of surprise "Oh" and naturalness "Of course" that I have come to associate with invitations of the Spirit.

I wrote the words at the top of my notes, sensing that whatever had moved could easily slip below the surface of my awareness. Something vital resided in them for my own wholeness and for my capacity as a director tending the movements of Spirit in others. Several years before I had experienced — and said a reflexive "No!" to — the disturbing approach of a God who wanted an intimacy that scared me. I still grieved that "No" and my inability to welcome what I most deeply wanted. At the same time, I was becoming aware of how much life I experienced in conversations with directees — and of a palpable intimacy growing in our times as we touched the depths of sacred story together.

I had noticed too that, while my practice as a director in a local congregation was burgeoning and conversation was broad as well as deep, nobody talked about matters of sexuality. Well, not explicitly. Many of my directees made references to abuse histories or struggles with relationships that they were typically working through in therapy, but "sex" as an identifiable topic stayed outside the direction room. I wondered why and whether it mattered.

Mostly I experienced awe in listening to the lives of directees — a felt sense of taking off my shoes and standing with them on holy ground. Occasionally, however, other feelings intruded. When a male directee brought a dream about me into a session, I felt a mild excitement followed by guarded self-annoyance. When he later told his wife — and then me — that he felt like he was committing "spiritual adultery" by sharing his soul with me in direction, it provoked an altogether different response: I panicked internally wondering what I had done wrong.

Energies of relatedness, intimacy, desire, mutuality, generative life, and the urge toward wholeness, as well as places of incapacity, injury, and distortion within and among all parties in the direction relationship point to the sacred fire — Eros — at the core of the human person. Something like the laddered strands of the DNA double helix, sexuality and spirituality are intimately tied together. We cannot have one without the other.[71]

Our programs for forming directors need to prepare candidates for their own awakening and growth toward psycho-sexual-spiritual integration as well as for recognizing and responding to the interpersonal energies that will be part of spiritual unfolding within the direction relationship. Beyond the interpersonal, many commentators note what appears to be a historical moment in human history that invites expanded consciousness. Because spiritual and sexual energies are so primal and interconnected, any large movements of human awakening will likely be accompanied by surging sexual impulses that need to be carefully discerned and integrated.

Powerful energies, especially in times of passage, need conscious tending. Ronald Rolheiser reminds us that "energy, especially sexual energy, is not always friendly and it often seeks to take us across borders prematurely or irreverently."[72] Reverent, wakeful tending is a necessary antidote to both the contemporary naiveté about the power and nature of erotic and creative energy as well as to a reflexive fear that seeks to repress the pulse of life itself. Three important aspects of preparation for director/guides are exposure to a theology of sexuality, an experience of reflecting on one's own sacred sexual story, and the opportunity to engage in casework with peers that will give practical experience in approaching the energies that arise in the direction relationship. All of these modes assist in developing the capacity to hold "the most powerful of all fires, the best of all fires, the most dangerous of all fires, and the fire which ultimately lies at the base of everything, including the spiritual life."[73]

Toward a Theology of Sexuality

Honoring what is life-giving while respecting what is dangerous about the sacred fire at the human core requires more than rules. Diarmuid O'Murchu notes that the spiritual landscape rather than religious tradition is the contemporary arena for theological exploration and opens up new horizons of possibility and ultimate meaning[74] while providing a framework for right relationship.

The experience of mystics and saints across traditions and generations reveals the spiritual-sexual landscape in ways that are remarkably similar and which point toward the metaphor of the Divine Lover who draws the beloved ever closer. The Hebrew Scriptures repeatedly portray the human-divine relationship in the love language of the joyful intimate "knowing" of covenanted spouses. In this vein, the Baal Shem Tov, Polish mystic and founder of the Hassidic movement, comments on Job 19:26, "Yet from my flesh I shall see God" (NAS): "Just as you cannot sire [a child] in physical copulation unless your organ is 'alive' and [you are filled with] desire and joy, so it is with spiritual coupling, that is, with regards to the words of Torah and prayer: when it is done with a live organ, in joy and pleasure, then you can be fecund."[75]

The goodness of the bodied life and capacity to enjoy the sensory pleasures that are God's good gift to humanity are similarly reflected in the Talmudic declaration "You will be held accountable [in the World to Come] for every legitimate pleasure you denied yourself!"[76] So, too, Christian and Muslim mystics who enter the waters of transforming relationship with the Holy find themselves relying on metaphors of intense spiritual-sensual longing and love. Even Augustine, whose legendary struggles with sexuality have left a deep mark on Christian theology, used the lush language of the senses to express his relationship with God: "You called, you cried, you shattered my deafness. You sparkled, you blazed, you drove away my blindness. You shed your fragrance, and I drew in my breath and I pant for you. I tasted and now I hunger and thirst. You touched me, and now I burn with longing for your peace."[77]

In the same way that the spiritual expresses in sexual language, the sexual points to spirit. Phillip Yancey, an evangelical Christian, names sex as "probably the loudest single rumor of another world that most people ever experience. It's the closest thing to transcendence that people feel. It's a powerful force that seems irresistible — there's nothing that pulls a person out of himself or herself more than sexual attraction to another being. What concerns me is that most people think of sex and God as polar opposites. If it's the most powerful force that most people experience, then to me it's a pointer."[78]

I would add that the experience of sexual attraction as well as its consummation in the faithful sharing of intimate life also points toward generative participation within the outer "bodies" of communal and cultural life. Spirituality is not only about interiority, but also about relatedness. One of the Spirit's primary invitations in this time is, I believe, movement toward living the undivided life. Individually that might include healing the split between body and spirit or corporately moving toward participative integration of the personal and social life.

The urge to live a life of growing integrity extends also to a deeper moral agency seeking to arise so that moral behaviors are not just put on from the outside, but flow from the interior heart of the person and society, enabling self-donating love to flow outward. There are many apparent dualisms warring in our time that are actually polarities seeking a new way of being in relationship — a communion perhaps — that honors the rightful place of each without being held captive by either.

To be sexed is to be in the state of separation that precedes communion, and to be irresistibly attracted to the other. The Latin root
of the word "sex" comes from *secare* meaning to be cut off, severed,
amputated, or disconnected from the whole.[79] The sexing of humanity in the archetypal separation of Eve from Adam points to the long
journey into awakening as separate selves with the potential to freely
choose reconnection in love. Leaving behind an unconscious and primal union with God and within humanity (first experienced in our
mother's womb) opens the possibility of authentic mutuality and intimacy in communion. To be sexed is to be separate and to be alive
with restless energies that drive toward reconnection.

These restless energies are embedded in the erotic nature of creation itself from the atoms that unite to form elements, to the pulsing
energies in the halls of a high school, to the poetry of the mystics. The
Sufi poet Hafiz attributed our separation from the "warm body" of
God as a source of our constant yearning. Cosmologist Brian Swimme
refers to the power of attraction that saturates the universe as "cos-
mic allurement."[80] In human experience we call this relational power
love, and sexual energy at its best is the embodied expression of
that love. We are made to move out toward the other. The only issue
is how — in honor of self and other or as objects of gratification:
"Sexuality is a beautiful, good, extremely powerful sacred energy,
given us by God and experienced in every cell of our being as an
irrepressible urge to overcome our incompleteness, to move toward
unity and consummation with that which is beyond us. It is also
the pulse to celebrate, to give and receive delight, to find our way
back to the Garden of Eden where we can be naked, shameless, and
without worry and work as we make love in the moonlight. Ultimately though, all these hungers, in their full maturity, culminate in
one thing: They want to make us co-creators with God. Sexuality is
not simply about finding a love or even finding a friend. It is about
overcoming separateness by giving life and blessing it. Thus, in its
maturity, sexuality is about giving oneself over to community, friendship, family, service, creativity, humor, delight, and martyrdom, so
that, with God, we can help bring life into the world."[81]

Awakening to the Sacred Sexual Self

Movement from theology to personal story is crucial grounding for the director-to-be. Healthy sexuality and spirituality are embodied; they incarnate in human experience. Edwin McMahon and Peter Campbell comment that "after years of experience as therapists, we have found that the single most damaging Christian influence impeding psycho-sexual development is the inherited piety of 'personal relationship to Jesus.' Too often such piety simply provides an easily available religious escape hatch for avoiding the risks and responsibilities of sexual integration. Instead of growing through the pain and fear of intimate human encounter, a relationship with a sexually safe and disembodied Jesus can be substituted."[82]

My formation program colleagues and I intentionally weave multiple experiences of body prayer and movement into all our processes to assist in waking up and grounding "in the flesh." This is also true of multiple passes at the theme of sacred story. As directors, we will be able to tend the sacred fire in others to the degree we are open to exploring it in ourselves. This includes becoming aware of the sexual dimension of our own sacred history as well as assumptions, attitudes and values about both sex and sexuality. A powerful tool for wading into these waters in the formation program is to have the directors-to-be write a graced history that focuses on their psychosexual unfolding.

Psychosexual development, according to Fran Ferder and John Heagle, is another term for "growing up" in our relational lives, and they view it as a pathway to love, not just a behavioral process. Growth toward psychosexual integration reveals four qualities that underlie human and sexual development: (1) emerging self-awareness, (2) responsible freedom, (3) developing creativity, and (4) deepening capacity for intimacy.[83] Our psycho-sexual story reveals "all the moments of growth, excitement, discovery, pain, struggle, and questioning in our relational lives. This is the story of our growing up — our journey toward friendship and human communion. It is the story of our physical and emotional awakenings, our yearnings and our fantasies, our soaring feelings and our broken hearts, our desires and our dependencies, our struggles with shame and our breakthroughs to mutuality."[84]

Ferder and Heagle use a four-part process for initiating the exploration of sacred sexual story. The only guidelines are to listen to our own story with openness, honesty, and reverence. First, they use the journaling device called "Stepping Stones" developed by Ira Progoff, to outline major turning points or transition experiences. Specifically, they ask, "What are 7 or 8 key stepping stones in your psychosexual story and what do they reveal about your search for love and intimacy?" Second, "What were the core life messages about sexuality — verbal or nonverbal — in your family?" Third, "Who are the persons who have helped you come to a more affirming understanding of sexuality and intimacy?" Fourth, "What would you like to reimage or reinterpret in your attitudes and inherited messages toward sexuality?"[85] The journaler is asked to jot down reflections and to bring them to prayer and to someone they trust, a wonderful foundation and opening for a fledgling director.

Supporting the Practice

A statement of guidelines to use when listening to the sexual stories of our directees, along with case examples that can be discussed with peers and in reflection papers for the mentor, is very helpful. It gives program staff multiple views of the development of the intern and opens the field for the interns to explore possible responses to "live" situations.

Many of these guidelines were first presented by Janet Ruffing, RSM, and Don Bisson, FMS, for the Spiritual Directors International Symposium, *Expanding Our Horizons: Toward a Renewed Sexuality,* in 1998. The single case outlined here is intended to give a taste of the kind of material that might be helpful. The reflection questions at the end of this piece can be used as a further tool to help interns and staff explore the topic.

Some Guidelines and Reminders

1. Hold a Broad Frame

Sexuality is never just about sex, and spirituality is never just about spirit. Both are often coded material about emergent issues of personhood. Our sexuality is about much more than our genitals and what we do or don't do with them; it's also about our bodies and senses, self-perceptions, relationships, creativity, the ways we connect and are generative in the world. Remembering the broad frame helps a director to receive material and explore it as we do any other material for the presence of God.

Here is a case example to be followed by group reflection with the four questions at the end of this section: A directee, a single woman in her late forties in ministry in the church, has been deepening in her relationship with God. One day she comes to direction and after a significant pause says, "There's something I need to tell you. It's really embarrassing and I've never told anyone this before. I'm afraid of what you'll think of me." There's another long pause. "We've talked before about how hard it is for me to have any sort of a social life in the church. Well, there's a way I've kind of created one for myself. Late at night when I'm all alone, I go into the online chat rooms where I can pretend to be anyone I want to be. I know it sounds stupid, but it's kind of exciting. Lately the conversations are getting more and more suggestive sexually, so I know I need to stop it, but part of me enjoys it. Don't get me wrong, I have no desire to actually meet these people, but it lets me pretend for a little while that there's more to my life than just work."

2. Desire is Primary

Desire is primary to both spirituality and sexuality and to the formation of the human person. Part of the director's role is to encourage the voicing and exploration of the directee's longing for intimacy, which includes naming these desires to God. Intimacy is not necessarily about genitality, but about being a revealed self before a

revealed other. Exploring what the directee wants and the willingness to embrace the changes or implications that would result is a
door to the deeper realms. Questions that point toward the possibility of mutuality — "Is there any sense of God's desire for you?" may
also be fruitful.

3. Awakening of the Body and Senses

An awakening of the body and senses will occur as the person deepens in relationship with God. This can be alarming to the directee and
to the director unless it is held in the broader frame of spiritual awakening. The surging energies of bodily awakening can flood the sexual
centers of body and mind so powerfully that it seems the opposite
of spiritual experience. It is, however, a deeply spiritual movement
of incarnation which is gradually integrated into the whole person.
Part of our task as directors is to help the directee experience the
awakening arousal and bring it with consciousness to the primary
relationship with God. The director may also assist in making a distinction between having an experience and moving into action in the
world.[86]

4. The Stance of Active Love and Compassion

Hold the stance of love and compassion with and for the directee. We
must consciously resist being the moral enforcers of tradition. Join-
ing directees in their struggles and ambiguities requires nothing less
than enduring the tension of God-at-work. Becoming comfortable
with "mistake making" and learning as part of the human process is
necessary, as is the understanding that a director is not responsible
for the choices a directee makes. This is not about being morally neutral; rather, it is about going morally deeper by enabling an authentic
moral agency to arise internally in a conversion of heart. What initially presents as moral laxity or seeming infidelity may ultimately
be an opening to new depth as the person seeks to become a "true I
before a true thou."

5. Supervision

Supervision is crucial for holding the energies and for growth in freedom as we sit with directees in whatever sexual/spiritual experience they bring. God meets directees where they are, not where we are. The director needs to remain conscious and reflective about feelings and judgments related to the directee's relational choices so that they don't interfere with the directee's freedom. If we're tempted to close what is uncomfortable with the "right" answer or to become the teacher, that's a signal that we're seeking our own comfort rather than listening in service of the directee.

6. Heat, Passion, and Transformation

Heat and passion are necessary for transformation, and they can be dangerous. Spirituality flourishes in true vulnerability in which old self and God images come apart and open to the More of Spirit. When entering the depths with another, directors and directees alike experience intimacy and vulnerabilities. Add to this the presence of explicitly sexual content, and both intimacy and vulnerability soar. So do the potential gifts and possibility of real transformation. Rolheiser reminds us that sex "is not just like anything else, despite our culture's protest. Its fire is so powerful, so precious, so close to the heart and soul of a person, and so godly, that it either gives life or it takes it away. It can never be casual, but is either a sacrament or a destructive act."[87] As directors, we need to be both welcoming and wise in tending this sacred energy.

Walking this way with directors in formation is sacred travel in which we affirm by our attention and intention that sexuality is not a problem to be solved but a mystery to be welcomed and lived. Hildegard of Bingen celebrates what she calls *veriditas* or the lush, greening power of God in our lives and world. In the face of God's flowing lushness, she believed that the only true sin is to dry up.[88] May our students awaken to the vital importance of staying both juicy and on fire in their own lives and in their capacity to welcome the fully alive human person that Irenaeus of Lyons calls "the glory of God."

For Further Reflection

1. What do you notice in yourself as you read the situation described in the case study included here? What inner "movements" do you experience toward and away from him/her; toward and away from his/her experience?

2. How might you as director respond?

3. What attitudes, values and personal experiences might affect your response?

4. How free would you be to work with him/ her as a spiritual director?

Resources

Cameli, Louis J., Fran Ferder, Anthony Gittins, John Heagle, and Thomas Groome. *Imagining a New Church: Building a Community of Life.* Notre Dame, Ind.: Ave Maria Press, 2003.

Davis, Avram. "Kabbalah, Sexuality, and the Body," *Gnosis Magazine* (Fall 1993).

Evans, Donald. *Spirituality and Human Nature.* Albany, N.Y.: SUNY Press, 1992.

Ferder, Fran, and John Heagle. *Tender Fires: The Spiritual Promise of Sexuality.* New York: Crossroad, 2002.

———. *Your Sexual Self: Pathway to Authentic Intimacy.* Notre Dame, Ind.: Ave Maria Press, 1992.

Fox, Matthew. *Illuminations of Hildegard of Bingen.* Santa Fe, N.Mex.: Bear and Company, 1985.

Halligan, Fredrica, and John Shea. *The Fires of Desire: Erotic Energies and the Spiritual Quest.* New York: Crossroad, 1992.

Hillman, J. *The Soul's Code: In Search of Character and Calling.* New York: Random House, 1996.

McMahon, Edwin, and Peter Campbell. *A Biospiritual Approach to Sexuality: Healing a Spirituality of Control.* Kansas City, Mo.: Sheed and Ward, 1991.

Nelson, James B. *Between Two Gardens: Reflection on Sexuality and Religious Experience.* New York: Pilgrim Press, 1983.

O'Murchu, Diarmuid. *Reclaiming Spirituality.* New York: Crossroad, 1998.

———. *Quantum Theology.* New York: Crossroad, 1997.

Rolheiser, Ronald. *The Holy Longing: The Search for a Christian Spirituality.* New York: Doubleday, 1999.

Ruffing, Janet. *Spiritual Direction: Beyond the Beginnings.* Mahwah, N.J.: Paulist Press, 2000.

Sewell, Laura. "Earth, Eros, Sky." *Earthlight* (Winter 2000–2001); an essay excerpted from her book *Sight and Sensibility: The Ecopsychology of Perception* (New York: Tarcher/Putnam, 1999).

Sheldrake, John. *Befriending Our Desires.* Notre Dame, Ind.: Ave Maria Press, 1994.

Swimme, Brian. *The Universe Is a Green Dragon.* Santa Fe, N.Mex.: Bear and Company, 1985.

Timmerman, J. *Sexuality and Spiritual Growth.* New York: Crossroad, 1993.

Ulanov, Ann, and Barry Ulanov. *Primary Speech: A Psychology of Prayer.* Atlanta: John Knox Press, 1982.

———. *The Healing Imagination: The Meeting of Psyche and Soul.* New York: Paulist Press, 1991.

Washburn, Michael. *Transpersonal Psychology in Psychoanalytic Perspective.* Albany, N.Y.: SUNY Press, 1994.

Welwood, John. *Love and Awakening: Discovering the Sacred Path of Intimate Relationship.* New York: HarperCollins, 1997.

———. *Journey of the Heart: The Path of Conscious Love.* New York: HarperCollins, 1996.

Yancey, Philip, "Sex, Lies, and Life on the Evangelical Edge." Interview with Jim Wallis, *Sojourner's Magazine* (February 2004): *www.sojo.net/index.cfm?action=magazine.*

Who Am I? Who Are You?

Gender Issues in the Formation of Directors

One of the most important issues we deal with as spiritual directors is gender. Questions of who we are as men and as women, how societal and religious institutions have socialized us because of our gender, and even who God is (gendered, ungendered, male, female, or other) draws us onto holy — and often confusing — broken ground. Therefore, we must deal with gender issues with great sensitivity, always seeking to grow in our awareness of how gender colors and shapes who we are as children of God.

We all face the challenge not to fall into stereotypical language or assumptions about women and men. Each culture has gender stereotypes and biases, and we unconsciously bring these with us into the direction relationship. It is not always obvious, but our relationships with God are directly affected by our concepts and language of human relationships. So gender issues are also often very much spiritual issues.

Emphasis on the Common Journey

In my work on gender issues, I often team up with Kathleen Geelan, a psychiatric nurse, spiritual director, supervisor, mother, and grandmother. We present issues that might impact the direction relationship from a male/female perspective. But always, before we share the unique issues faced by men and women, we find it important to illustrate what women and men have in common on the spiritual journey.

We are all called to a journey in, through, with, and to God. This is always a risky journey into the unknown. God loves both men and women unconditionally, yet we often resist this intimacy and sabotage the very relationship with the Holy that we desire. All of us pass through various stages of development and growth, seeking healing and wholeness. We need one another on this journey because we know that we can't do it alone. We seek consolation, support, and wisdom. As men and women, we enter into periods of darkness, breakthroughs, and breakdowns. We are all called to conversion, to move from self-alienation toward unity with the Divine. Surrender is always fearful and change is ambivalent. We grow through self-knowledge and self-disclosure, both of which are risky but transformative.

Though these sacred callings are similar for both men and women, the ways they are manifested can be quite different. To help recognize and understand these different manifestations, let's look at some distinctive issues for men and women that may have an impact on our spiritual lives.

Specific Issues of Women and Men

Through his book with a similar title, John Gray popularized the idea that men are from Mars, and women are from Venus. Gray examined ways men and women differ in key areas of experience such as relationships, work, and communication. Coming at these differences from a slightly different direction, I would like now to suggest a few issues for women and men that may affect the direction process.

Women's Issues

I'll start first with an apology — that I'm using the third person in this section. It sounds a bit distant, but I don't presume (or want to imply) that I can express women's issues from experience. Instead, I rely here on the wisdom and experience of the women trainers with whom I work. They emphasize five areas of women's issues, which seem to be reinforced by the literature.

First, women need to find their own voice and trust more deeply in their own experience. They need to honor feminine ways of knowing through intuition and feeling as a valid way of being in relationship with God and others. Women need to be listened to with reverence and respect, so that they can be "listened into" strength and new life. Speaking her truth and overcoming a deadening silence helps transform a woman's relationship to herself and to God.

This moves us into the second area, in which women rediscover their personal authority and personal power from their experience. This helps women identify their power in society, thus allowing them to challenge unjust structures in family, church, community, the workplace, and in the political arena.

Third, women are invited to reclaim their bodies as sacred and to see themselves as manifestations of God's creation. They must detoxify the objectification of the female body — of their own bodies — in our culture, which leads to shame and guilt. Because women often have suffered from many forms of abuse, spiritual direction can become a safe place, a haven of compassion and healing. Because women's relationships with God often have been shattered by abusive relationships, spiritual direction can also help heal their relationship to the Sacred.

Fourth, women need to own their limits and needs. Since women are naturally relational, caring for others' needs supersede caring for their own. Without necessary boundaries and self-care, women deplete themselves personally, physically, and spiritually. Knowing one's limits can be a new form of liberation.

Finally, an area in which feminist theology has been very helpful is the exploration of new images of God and reinterpretation of Scripture, which enables women to reconnect with their traditions in a new, life-giving way. Two women theologians who have been very helpful in this area are Sallie McFague in her book *Models of God* and Elizabeth Johnson in *She Who Is*. These are not only useful for women but also for men seeking new avenues to God.

Men's Issues

First, a key challenge in men's spiritual lives is the dichotomy we experience between doing and being. Social conditioning encourages us to identify with performance at work, in the family, and in the bedroom. We have a natural competitiveness, which distracts and diminishes movement in the spiritual life.

Second, we are programmed to deny feelings and value thoughts. This leads to a distrust of, and even an antagonism toward, feelings of vulnerability, neediness, love, grief, and tenderness. Conditioned to express feeling through anger, we often have difficulty differentiating other, more subtle, feelings. We feel shamed by our feelings rather than seeing them as expressions of the complexity of life. This uneasiness with feelings can be a challenge in the spiritual direction relationship because the unveiling of God stirs up so many feelings and emotions.

Third, like women, we men have body issues, but they are of a different sort. We spend so much time in our heads that we're barely aware of the rest of our bodies — it's as if we cut ourselves off at the neck, holding onto the head and letting everything else go. We deny the needs of our bodies, which paradoxically can lead to addictive behaviors and illness associated with denial. Through sports, work, and peer relationships, we learn that to pay attention to body needs is not "manly." Physical exertion, pumping iron, inviting pain toughens us and increases our tolerance for discomfort, which is necessary for success in life. As boys, many of us experienced verbal, sexual, and physical abuse from both men and women. The stereotype that men can't be, or aren't allowed to be, victims often interferes with the possibility of healing. Both psychotherapy and spiritual direction may be necessary to unravel the lies and half-truths of conditioning.

Fourth, homophobia is rampant in our society. This fear of those who are gay and the fear of being (or being identified as) gay underlies many problems that we adult males encounter when moving into new places in our spiritual lives. We may resist spiritual direction itself because, for the most part, we only see women seeking out direction. Many men, I've found, are more open to direction after a men's retreat or some other formative experience that helps them articulate their desire for God. Homophobia also blocks intimacy with ourselves as we deny the feminine within; it distorts friendships with both men and women, and it limits our freedom to express deep affective feelings for God in the person of Jesus.

Finally, we men generally keep our spiritual lives in the closet. We may feel more comfortable talking about religion or God than having a relationship with God. Because we are oriented to fixing things, being concrete, and achieving at work and in the world, we often find spiritual direction very challenging because in direction we begin to recognize and share movements that previously were unconscious and unknown. We feel threatened because we are not in control, and may experience this powerlessness as failure rather than simple reality.

As human beings — men and women — we are challenged to move out of our conditioned responses to greater human freedom and intimacy with the God who loves us as we really are. The experience of direction — both as directors and directees — can help guide us in this movement toward fuller life.

Masculine and Feminine Approaches in Spiritual Direction

Approaches to spiritual direction, though not gender specific, may be masculine or feminine. Recognizing our own preferred approach as directors is just as important as it is to recognize the preference of our directees.

From experience, I find that the masculine-insight approach is preferred by most men and some women, and the feminine-feeling approach is preferred by most women and some men. Our preference emerges from our educational experiences, personality type, and social conditioning. For many years, I was unaware of the different approaches. They became clear to me one day when I met with a directee, a man, who had an insight-driven mode of pursuing direction. Then, immediately following him, I met with a directee, a woman, with a feeling approach. I found myself adjusting my own direction approach in response to their ways of spiritual seeking. Let's look a little closer now at these two approaches — insight and feeling — and how they affect our work as directors.

When an "insight" directee (a man or a woman) comes to spiritual direction, he shares his thoughts, readings, and reflections from the past month. These are significant for him and have a spiritual "pull" that is important to acknowledge. He is not necessarily stuck in his head or in resistance but rather is sharing what has heart and meaning in his spiritual story. He is neither prepared to share his feelings nor to access emotional stirrings at this point. We delve into his insights, staying with what seems to attract and have energy. The art here is in staying and going deeper till there is a shift leading to an "ah-ha," an awakening to God at work. This leads to an emotional release or a deeper silence. The revelation of God at work unites his insight with an embodied affect. The connection of life experience, God, and new meaning touches his soul.

Let's look at what might happen in a direction session with an insight-driven directee.

- Directee Number One arrives wanting to discuss a book he has been reading called *Palace to Nowhere,* with the insights about the true and false self. He is intrigued and wants to know more; he is seeking what he most desires.

- I begin to probe with him what insights grabbed his attention, noticing the energy and what seems to be repeated, probing as to why he comes back to this theme. Where is this energy coming from?

- He begins to speak of his own life and how he is wrestling with his false self at work, how he cannot be as true as when he comes to direction.

- I begin to probe, seeking God's revelation in the differences he finds in himself.

- He begins to see these dynamics and feels them in a powerful way. He is moved by God's work in him. He begins to recognize the call to manifest his true God self wherever he is, even at work.

- The emotions arrive and confirm his truth.

When a "feeling" directee (a woman or a man) comes to spiritual direction, she shares stirrings, feelings, and emotional vulnerability, which may include tears. She may not have conscious connections to what lies behind these feelings, but she knows — and as directors we need to recognize — that these emotions are an avenue for discovering both significance and meaning in her life experience. She is not resisting or avoiding insights behind her feelings; she simply experiences the feelings first. We stay with her feelings and emotions, and go deeper into the story surrounding them. Insight into her experiences emerges and grows, and she experiences an "ah-ha" as she recognizes the power of God at work in her life. Her feelings are integrated with insight from her reflection.

Here's what might happen in a direction session with a feeling-driven directee.

- Directee Number Two arrives, and within a few minutes, she is in tears. She feels disturbed emotionally and can't get a handle on what is happening or why she is experiencing so much frustration.

- We stay with the feelings and begin to let them arrive, since they are not of sorrow but of confusion and anger. She notices that she has been holding on to these feelings for a while, and now in direction she is free to be her true self and allow herself the freedom to be.

- While probing into her life experience, she realizes that she is holding on to these feelings because she has to be "shut down" at work. She cannot be herself or speak her truth. She realizes she is being false, and it feels terrible.

- These insights allow her to experience anger in a healthy way. She senses she is being called to remain in her true self with God no matter the cost. She leaves with new confidence, empowered by her insight.

Gender Issues and Training Directors

As we train directors, we cannot train for only one approach because directees will come to us with both preferences. Since female directees and trainers predominate, so does the feminine-feeling approach. We must, however, be careful not to assume that this approach, because it is more common, is more spiritual, more mature, and/or less resistant. Directees whose preference differs from ours will challenge us and move us out of our comfort zones, and thereby provide important material for us to consider with our direction supervisor, especially if we are doing shadow work (e.g., with the material of the unconscious that arises in direction as well as therapy), or with an opposite type (e.g., director is an extrovert; directee is introverted).

In presenting gender issues, whenever possible, it is important to have a male-female team teach from their personal experiences. It's also important to be aware that interns may vary widely in their exposure to, understanding of, and comfort with gender issues. Some, for instance, may be well versed in feminist theology, insight, and language, while others have never been exposed to this material and thought. Age, culture, education, and other variables influence gender issues and responses to them. Some women have great knowledge in women's issues and but little awareness of male psychology and spirituality. Most men have difficulty naming their unique challenges. Because of this, real play or role-play can help formation program participants to actually see and experience gender issues as they might arise in a direction session.

Despite much good work on women's issues in spiritual direction (especially Kathleen Fisher's classic work *Women at the Well*), little has been done with men's issues. Much work remains to be done in this important area.

Throughout the training process, we will encounter the interplay of gender and spiritual direction over and over in group dynamics, sharing, and literature. As Genesis 1:26 reminds us, we — male and female — are made in the image of God. That commonality, the foundation of our humanity, is central to our spiritual quest despite gender, experiential, or any other kind of difference. In our work as directors, as well as in our own spiritual journeys, we are called to wholeness, growth, compassion, self-love, and love of the other as we are drawn deeper into the mystery of God.

For Further Reflection

1. How comfortable are you listening to gender issues with a person of a different gender?

2. What impact have your own gender issues had on your prayer and your own image of God?

3. What gender issues might be challenging for you to help another recognize and explore? Give concrete examples, particularly with directees, if possible.

4. How would you describe your insight modality as a directee?

Resources

Bisson, Donald. "Melting the Iceberg: Spiritual Direction for Men." *Parabola* 6, no. 2 (May 2000).

Dunne, Carrin. *Behold Woman: A Jungian Approach to Feminist Theology.* Wilmette, Ill.: Chiron Publications, 1990.

Dyckman, Katherine, M. Garwin, and E. Liebert. *The Spiritual Exercises Reclaimed: Uncovering Possibilities for Women.* Mahwah, N.J.: Paulist Press, 2001.

Fisher, Kathleen. *Women at the Well: Feminist Perspectives on Spiritual Direction.* Mahwah, N.J.: Paulist Press, 1988.

Gray, John. *Mars and Venus in the Workplace.* New York: HarperCollins, 2002.

Johnson, Elizabeth A. *She Who Is: The Mystery of God in Feminist Theological Discourse.* New York: Crossroad, 2000.

Johnson, Robert. *He: Understanding Masculine Psychology.* San Francisco: HarperSanFrancisco, 1997.

———. *She: Understanding Feminine Psychology.* San Francisco: HarperSanFrancisco, 1976.

Jung, Emma. *Animus and Anima.* Dallas: Spring Publications, 1981.

McFague, Sallie. *Metaphorical Theology: Models of God in Religious Language.* Philadelphia: Fortress Press, 1982.

Moore, Robert, and Douglas Gillette. *King, Warrior, Magician, Lover.* San Francisco: HarperSanFrancisco, 1990.

Rohr, Richard. *Quest for the Grail.* New York: Crossroad, 1994.

Sanford, John. *The Invisible Partners.* Mahwah, N.J.: Paulist Press, 1980.

Tacey, David. *Remaking Men: Jung, Spirituality, and Social Change.* New York: Routledge 1997.

GROUNDED IN
THE REAL

Surviving (and Thriving) as Supervisors
Some Dynamics of a Supervisory Program

When a practicum program in spiritual direction gets its head of steam and starts rolling, the psychological and spiritual change that begins to happen to individuals in a group can be alternately thrilling and terrifying. To those of us who serve as staff, it can sound like something horribly wrong with the engine unless we are prepared to listen beneath the noise to what is running smoothly all the time. To help us "listen beneath the noise," let's look at how we, as practicum staffs, may experience and handle two issues that arise in different ways in different programs, issues that we call the "personal-conversion phenomenon" and a "narcissistic crisis."

Many programs for developing spiritual directors are founded on strongly held assumptions about God, prayer, and spiritual life — assumptions that have usually been tried and found worthy. Because we can never finally capture the Mystery of God or the varieties of prayer, this stance will probably confront to some degree the spiritual lives of the participants. People will be challenged to confirm their own experience anew, to look into it more deeply than before, or to criticize and possibly jettison old assumptions about some of the most important things in life. This is usually an important and welcome development, signaling real engagement in the program. But it can sound and feel as if the train is getting derailed. Participants may discover the inadequacy of former spiritual directors or may encounter their need for counseling or therapy. Anger may arise and be projected onto staff, peers, friends, or especially directees. The Spirit of God may be knocking, wanting to be let out of the box.

135

The Personal-Conversion Phenomenon

Since participants often experience the "personal-conversion phenomenon," it can become a group issue. We may best address this
if there is in place some group function where participants are encouraged to talk with one another about what is happening to them
personally. A valuable instrument for this is contemplative dialogue,
which provides a set of tools to help participants look more clearly
and lovingly at what is before them: to notice the way that inferences
can separate us instantly from reality, and to notice and bring forth
their assumptions about a particular issue, suspending them before
the group and asking for conversation about them. So a person may
say how annoyed he is that people go out of their way to desexual-
ize their language about God. He might discover that his assumption
was that such language is an example of politically correct speech
and should not be brought into play in spiritual direction. The en-
suing conversation may reveal to him the limits to that assumption,
and that others use "laundered language" to point intentionally to
the Mystery of an unfathomable God. As the conversation goes on,
other assumptions will probably surface and need conversation; e.g.,
that it is important for a director to stay with a directee's language
rather than to try, however subtly, to judge or change it.

Contemplative dialogue does not end with someone winning the
argument, another losing. Ideally, it should end with everyone being
heard and recognized as having an important piece of the truth of the
whole group. A new awareness may emerge of who we are, we who
make up this group. Often a larger truth may come forward from the
group, larger than any of the topics addressed. Thus, one evening at
the end of ninety minutes of contemplative dialogue, someone spoke
the group mind when she said, "It strikes me that we're going to be
forever a community of learners because God is too big to get trapped
in any of our categories."

Finally, participants' conversion experiences can be so strong and
so generally felt that, unless we expect and understand it, the opera-
tive goal of the program can subtly shift from ministerial to personal

growth. This can happen if we don't keep the emphasis on the work to be done, always conscious of helping the participants to bring their personal growth to bear on their work with directees. Here we ourselves may well need supervision. Elements of the program can be imperceptibly skewed away from the pastoral issues central to it. Because the person of the director is the focus of supervision, for instance, supervisory sessions may subtly become therapeutic rather than ministerial.

We might spend almost all of our sessions for the last month on the intern's relationship with members of his family. We neglect to spend much time exploring how this learning is impacting his or her work with directees. When this occurs, we have lost an opportunity to help the intern integrate his or her personal growth into a component of service to the ministry of spiritual direction. As supervisors, we must pay attention to this tendency to shift away from the focus on the pastoral component of this work.

If participants are consistently asked to consult their own experience of life or prayer in reflecting on their work, they may not develop the ability to remember and look critically at other people's experience, which offers them a wider and more surprising range. Material can be presented in a way that favors the participants' personal absorption of it and neglects the further step of reflecting on it in light of what they have seen in their directees. For example, the intern might read the works of Teresa of Ávila. In a practicum, it is not enough to read just to know the works of Teresa, but interns must be challenged to consider where they have seen anything like what Teresa has described in their work as a spiritual directors.

Further, we may need to be flexible enough to modify the syllabus or calendar, to adjust the presentation of material to the ability of individuals in the group to hear and absorb it.

The Narcissistic Crisis

The second issue, for which I borrow the term "narcissistic crisis,"[89] occurs in some form in most clinical programs and is complicated by the highly personal and value-laden religious material of spiritual direction. People tend to enter such programs with some infection from the cultural stereotype of the spiritual director as wise, holy, and powerful. Whether they measure themselves positively or negatively against this icon and its expectations, participants very often exhibit regressive behavior when a supervisor starts to look at the details of their work.

Initial confidence or self-doubt may turn into their opposites when otherwise successful and competent people find themselves scrutinized as they assume their new roles as supervised learners. For our purposes, it is important to notice that (1) participants may extraordinarily and unrealistically accept or challenge the foundational elements and philosophy of the program; (2) this is an expectable and welcome development, rather than something to be avoided, and demands our understanding, unity, and participation; and (3) this "narcissistic crisis" is primarily an individual issue (in that it will configure itself quite differently in each person's experience), but it can easily — and erroneously — be generalized into a broader dissatisfaction with the program when it catches similar issues in other participants.

The resistance of this phase of practicum training often sounds like rebellion or despair: "I've heard all this before." "I am never going to do this right." "There are lots of ways of doing spiritual direction that you're not giving us." "Tell me what I should have said to this directee." At heart these are often statements about the personal difficulties individuals are encountering as their self-esteem experiences some dismantling in supervision or in their comparing themselves with more polished performances from peers or the staff. So we must be keen not to confuse them with genuine criticism or real understanding of the program's foundational elements. This resistance, when felt by a group (either the participants or the staff), can swamp and drown gentler voices of moderation and carries within itself strong "we versus them" projections that we must understand and treat as such lest they polarize the program. As supervisors, we need to look beneath the manifest behavior to the personal and professional issues that are awakening.

Successful negotiation of this "crisis" can be difficult for a staff, testing its team cohesiveness with urges to side with or against certain participants, and its willingness to recognize and respond flexibly to genuine criticism. Supervisors may be idealized, identified with, then ignored or renounced — made into idols and then melted down! Erosion of our own self-esteem and professional identity can tempt us to clear up a supervisee's anxiety and confusion rather than work with it as appropriate to this stage of learning, or perhaps to respond in anger, or to exaggerate or minimize the real demands of the program.

How to Survive as Supervisory Staff

The very survival of the supervisory staff may hinge upon our having done our work in two areas. First, a shared understanding of and desire to work with the foundational philosophy and pedagogy of the program is imperative and should not be taken for granted. Diversity of background and ideas can live together in a training program if all members of the staff are able to question it. New staffs need to put aside valuable time to discuss and haggle over what they mean by spiritual direction and training directors, and ongoing staffs could profit from a devil's advocate brought consciously into their midst.

Second, it is important that the supervisory work of each staff member be open to the others, at least to some degree. For the welfare of the program's participants and for the professional development of the staff, the work they do with participants ought itself to be supervised. It would be good to know and trust each other's work when some of the dynamics detailed here begin to operate, or at least to have a forum in which to challenge and hear one another.

If we maintain only a mentor's stance and never allow our own mistakes and biases to be dealt with, or if the program appears in-flexible, participants may perceive little room to blend what they have learned into their particular personalities. If the goal of a practicum is the integration of supervised learning into one's own personal style of doing spiritual direction, then the participants' success or failure in resolving this crisis could be crucial to their development as spiritual directors.

Failure might look like either a defensive posture against the program and its goals or a need to maintain one's connection with it in order to feel competent. On the other hand, a participant who finds support, challenge, and growing peership in supervision will probably grow away from dependence on the supervisor and the institution represented in the practicum. Toward the end of a successful year, for instance, a supervisee said with some force, "I'm going to park this whole damn program and get out and walk!" The remark, articulating his desire to integrate his learning with his own stride, would have told quite a different story — and been far less welcome — at the beginning of the year.

At some point any trained spiritual director, including ourselves, will have to question the basic principles of his or her training, experiment with them and integrate what is of substance into a personal, distinctive style of doing spiritual direction. A practicum can impart the skills and qualities needed in a spiritual director. A better practicum can aim to help qualified directors to be themselves in the practice of direction.

If we are able spiritual directors, we are women and men who have explored and become responsible for our own personalities and have, to some degree, integrated that with the ministry to which we have been called. We can dare to approach the intimate experience of another person and, above all, the Person of God, with humility and expectation. Before us is the task of reverencing the Mystery while exploring the everyday events in which the immeasurable personality of God becomes embodied.

For Further Reflection

1. Can you describe the philosophy of your formation program? How does the supervision practicum support the goals of the program?

2. What is the focus of a supervision session? Describe with specific examples.

3. As an intern, what are the most important qualities you hope to find in a supervisor?

4. How influential is your supervisor in your work as a spiritual director? Do you find yourself remembering supervisory sessions when you are directing?

Resources

Augsburger, David. *Caring Enough to Confront.* Glendale, Calif.: Regal Books, 1979.

Barry, William A., SJ, and Mary C. Guy, OSU. "The Practice of Supervision in Spiritual Direction." *Review for Religious* 37, no. 6 (1978): 834–42.

Conroy, Maureen, RSM. *The Discerning Heart: Discovering a Personal God.* Chicago: Loyola University Press, 1993.

———. *Looking into the Well.* Chicago: Loyola University Press, 1993.

Egan, Gerard. *The Skilled Helper: A Problem-Management and Opportunity-Development Approach to Helping.* Stamford, Conn.: Wadsworth Publishing, 2004.

Jorgensen, Susan. "Peer Supervision: One Model." *Presence* 2, no. 1 (January 1995): 23–38.

Whitehead, James D., and Evelyn Eaton Whitehead. *Method in Ministry.* New York: Seabury Press, 1981.

Wirth, Steven. "Reflections on Power Issues in the Training of Spiritual Directors." *Presence* 3, no. 1 (1997): 30–39.

www.contemplativedialogue.org.

Spiritual Direction in Community
Layers of Relationship

The energy level rises palpably in the room. The time has come for each participant in our formation program to announce availability as a director-intern to those in his or her community, and currents of anticipation and doubt move visibly across faces in the circle. A significant personal investment of time and resources toward engaging the practice of spiritual direction has already been made, yet a primary understanding of the formation programs of which I am a part is that spiritual companioning is a ministry that emerges from spiritual community and is confirmed by that community. Directees are not provided but emerge in response to a perceived gift. This does not mean, however, that all comers are appropriate.

Layers of Community Relationship

Besides assisting the fledgling director in listening for and setting the primary focus for the working covenant, careful attention needs to be given to layers of relationship within the context of community. Rather than adopting the distance model[90] of pure relationship uncontaminated by other types of contact (the reigning psychotherapeutic paradigm), ethical practice in spiritual direction focuses more on the question of how to cultivate safe connection within the living, breathing organism of communal relatedness. There are gifts this context of community bears and there are challenges. Degree of relationship as well as issues of power and responsibility can have an impact on the freedom needed for the primary work. Initial structural guidelines and a basis for ongoing discernment of relationship are needed as interns take mutually vulnerable first steps in opening to and selecting directees.

In her introduction to *Boundary Wars: Intimacy and Distance in Healing Relationships,* Katherine Hancock Ragsdale makes the bald statement, "Dual relationships are impossible to avoid in ministry."[91] Similarly the "Guidelines for Ethical Conduct" of Spiritual Directors International exhort directors to address "the difficulties multiple roles or relationships pose to the effectiveness or clarity of the spiritual direction relationship"[92] rather than to avoid them altogether. Both statements point to the structural realm of the lifeframe[93] or grid in a practice that is often perceived as occurring more in the interpersonal and intrapersonal realms. Awareness is the important first step, so it is important that a formation program explicitly describe and explore the structural issues and their impact for the sake of the potential directee, the new director, and the broader community.

In addition, while the initial discussion needs to set general parameters about focus, freedom, context, and degree of relationship, many subtleties emerge only with time and experience. My preference is to revisit the topic of ethics and relationship in the final year after interns have enough lived experience to distinguish between relational situations that truly hamper mutual freedom and those that are the Spirit's call to grow beyond a limited self-understanding. For example, a happy directee tells a friend about the value of spiritual direction and the friend contacts the director for an appointment. Rather than an automatic "never see friends" rule, the director might ask about the nature of the friendship and its relationship to the request for direction. Work in the context of spiritual community will always grow us beyond ourselves. Elements of teaching and discussion as well as times of corporate reflection on this topic speak to the ongoing formation and discernment that will necessarily be part of the practice across time.

What is a Dual Relationship?

What exactly is a dual relationship? Most easily described as mixed roles or the "wearing of more than one hat in a relationship," it occurs when the director and directee engage in a separate and distinct relationship alongside the direction relationship or within a reasonable period of time following its closure. In my own work as a spiritual director on the staff of a congregation, I experienced a duality as a leader in the community and director to the individual: "The roles might multiply from there to include any combination of spiritual director and liturgist, teacher, retreat leader, prayer group convener, formation group facilitator, or staff to governing boards. In this context I know and work with whole families and with networks of friends. Some of these settings appropriately involve some self-disclosure in the form of sharing my personal story or theology. Add to that the call for presence in the fellowship life of the community where we break bread together in church potlucks and mark the great life passages together in mourning or celebration."[94]

Engaging direction becomes possible to many precisely *because* the director is already known and perceived as one capable of "listening another's soul into a state of disclosure and discovery."[95] There is nothing more vulnerable than the sharing of soul. Knowing something about the director before beginning the work together helps establish a foundation of trust.

Yet this human relationship is only the vehicle for engagement. With a mutually covenanted focus on God, the primary container within which growth occurs is in the dynamic relationship between the directee and God. In this three-way partnership the role of the director is to serve as a focusing lens on the directee's unfolding relationship with the Holy. Assuring a "clean" space for noticing and responding to the movements of Spirit is crucial so that the touchstone of any mixing of roles is that it not compromise the effectiveness of this primary work.[96]

Parameters, Power, and Accountability

Thomas Hedberg and Betsy Caprio describe the commonly under-stood parameters of relationship where a personal investment exists or the unethical use of power in the relationship binds the radical freedom of directee and director to attend to the Spirit in their common work: "Prohibited, of course, is any covert or overt sexual intimacy or involvement between the two parties, or between the director and a directee's spouse or partner. Other types of dual relationships include socializing or business dealings with directees, direction relationships which flower into two-way friendships, bartering or exchanges of services, spiritual direction with one's friends, family members, students or supervisees, and directing close friends or more than one person from the same family."[97]

"The primary issue in these settings has to do with imbalance of power inherent in the structural role of director that can slide into using the vulnerability of the directee to fulfill personal needs and desires. Where power exists, good intentions are not enough; both consciousness and accountability are required. Even so, when the context of relationship is viewed as ministry of the community rather than as a professional compartment, to fail to protect is to put already hurt and vulnerable people at further risk. To overprotect is to deny adults the right to take the very risks that might set them free. People of good faith and informed judgment differ about which risks are worth taking, which are essential, and which are indefensible. The question, then, is how to decide what standards will govern our common life."[98]

Beyond the generally accepted boundaries noted above, the question she poses is the ongoing work of the community of accountability, contained initially within the formation program itself. We want — and need — to be *appropriately* protective, even as we realize that there is no ultimately and completely "safe" place except in God.

Now let's look at some guidelines that will be particularly helpful in dual relationships.

Guidelines for Dual Relationships

Guidelines can give a basis for choosing which relationships to enter and dynamics to monitor across time. They must also allow permeability for the work of the Spirit which is notorious for breaking out of even the best human boxes. Perhaps the way to engage the complexities of this issue is a statement of guidelines plus reliance on the peer or supervisory community for discerning the movement of the Spirit in a given situation.[99]

Focus of the Relationship

The relationship exists for the sole purpose of attending to the directee's unfolding relationship with God. Karen Lebacqz and Joseph Driskill assume that a directee approaches with a desire to develop his/her spiritual life more fully, a willingness to focus on the explicitly religious dimensions of life, and an acceptance of responsibility for spiritual growth.[100] This distinguishes the direction relationship from other forms of pastoral caregiving, including counseling. Clear guidance on focus in establishing the covenant for the work — what the direction relationship is and is not — assists the new director in avoiding another form of "dual relationship" that can be a particularly slippery slope. We live in an intensely therapeutic culture in which the distinctions between forms of caregiving too easily blur: "Both pastoral counseling and spiritual direction are forms of pastoral caregiving, but these forms have important structural differences: one focuses on healing, the other on growing; one meets more frequently, the other less; and in each process the dynamics of transference are focused differently. Whereas in pastoral counseling the transference onto the counselor is an important source of healing, in spiritual direction transference occurs in the relationship of the directee with the divine rather than with the human director."[101]

Freedom within the Focus

Avoiding obviously problematic dual relationships where competing interests collide and becoming clear about focus both lay the groundwork. Beyond this, for a solid director-directee relationship, sufficient internal and external freedom are needed to attend to the Spirit's presence and movement in life as well as to the human response to that presence and movement. The discernments become more subtle in this terrain because growth in human freedom is dynamic, developmental, and embedded within the shifting landscape of relationship in a communal context.

The directee needs to be free enough to come in radical openness, unfinishedness, and vulnerability to the Spirit in the presence of the director. The director needs to be free enough to come alongside the directee and listen, notice, and attend to how the Spirit is manifesting and what is evoked by the manifestations of the Spirit. The relationship is always in the service of the directee's unfolding relationship with the Holy.

Some structures of relationship and obstacles to freedom inherent in them include the following:

- *Relationships with the dimension of personal support or, even more subtly, of personal validation for, or caretaking of, the director may be problematic.*

A context where the director is known in other aspects of his or her life requires wakefulness and monitoring. Suppose that the director practices in a church where her battle with a chronic illness is common knowledge, and a recent request for prayer has been widely shared. While a directee may appropriately inquire how she is doing, is there an exaggerated concern about 'burdening' the director that makes the direction conversation suddenly more chatty and light? What if the directee is part of the church care team that delivers meals to the director's home?

In one sense, "support" belongs to the whole community, and yet awareness of the director's life situation can deflect the primary focus of the relationship if it becomes a source of concern to the directee. It's vital to healthy practice that a director have a personal system of support outside his/her directees, and use it.

One practice we engage during the formation process is asking interns to complete a monthly "situation sheet" that includes basic self-care. Two important questions are, "Describe the balance of work, rest, and play in your life this month" and "With which mutually nourishing relationship (where you are not the helper) did you intentionally spend quality time this month?" Attentiveness to one's own human needs for intimacy and support are a mutual protection.

- *Relationships where either director or directee is in a place of structural evaluation, oversight, or responsibility for the work of the other may interfere with the freedom of director and directee.*

The directee needs a place in which to open his or her heart freely. This is the *anamcara* or "soul friend" function of the director. The presence of an evaluative or gate-keeping function in which elements of personal judgment are necessarily present hampers the freedom of both parties to come in unbridled openness.

This awareness has implications for the formation program itself as well as for right selection of directees for new directors. As faculty in an internship program, we do not serve as directors to interns because we discern as a team about the viability of candidates. Even when an evaluation is positive, it changes the relationship into one in which potential for a negative evaluation is also present. Guardedness or censoring of the "unpretty" material in which the Spirit is often most active then becomes likely.

Interns need to pay attention to the various versions of the evaluative function in their particular setting as well. A minister or lay leader might legitimately work with members of his or her congregation or denomination as a spiritual director, but not if either one sits in a position of authority or responsibility for evaluating the work of the other.

For example, a congregation may have some version of a pastoral relations committee that evaluates staff, makes recommendations about salary, or discerns alongside clergy the future direction of the whole body. Imagine being a directee on such a committee when your director is the pastor. And imagine being the director knowing that the person with whom you sit has your future in his or her hands. Wherever an evaluative function exists, freedom to stand truly open-handed before the Spirit may be compromised by self-protection or fear of injuring the relationship.

Some of the evaluative tugs are easily recognizable and some are more subtle. One that intern-directors sometimes report has to do with their role as a learner. In a sense, the student-director needs the directee for practice and for discernment of call. Here the evaluative function is implicit to the process of discernment within the program, and a sense of need can leave the intern vulnerable to implied barter: "I am assisting you in meeting your requirement for this program, so maybe you can assist me with [my need or desire]." Clarity about the importance of keeping the relationship uncontaminated by considerations of need, debt, or guilt or anything other than what the Spirit is evoking can assist the intern in recognizing and resisting the temptation to keep the directee happy.

Ongoing Assessment

There are many gray areas that are best evaluated on a case-by-case basis. Serving together on committees is an example since there are different models used for their work.[102] One approach to the potential of impaired freedom in a direction relationship is to actively call on the gift of community through prayerful discernment with knowledgeable peers and/or one's supervisor in beginning a relationship and in monitoring its evolution across time.

The Director's Responsibility

It is the director's responsibility to state clearly what the spiritual direction relationship is and is not, and to acknowledge the multiple layers of relationship, their fluidity, and potential impacts. It is also the director's responsibility to invite mutual assessment of the dynamics of the relationship at periodic intervals. Simply asking, "When was the last time we talked specifically about this relationship and about whether there is anything that impedes our prayer and openness to the Spirit?" is a first step. Another is asking, "Does the nature of this relationship enhance mutual freedom or restrict it?" These questions assure that the relationship is one in which openness to the Spirit and mutual freedom are central.

In the formation program, this pattern can be set well before interns prepare for the initial interview. Asking them to write out their understanding of what they are engaging as they prepare for meeting with new directees is an important cross-check and basis for grounding the primary focus of the work. As potential directees come forward, the intern might submit to the program mentor a brief description of degrees and kinds of relationship that could impact freedom in the particular relationship, and commit to revisiting this quarterly. The direction relationship would then be continued, reshaped, or ended, as necessary.

Explicit attention to these foundational pieces can assist the intern in the initial interview and covenant-setting process. Simply naming the sorts of situations that might arise and ways of handling them can help the relationship stay clean. Suppose, for example, that the two are in the same congregation and a conflict erupts in which they find themselves on opposite sides. They might imagine together where that exploration might happen and with what degree of freedom.

Knowing that there is both "challenge" and "genius"[103] implicit in the communal context that holds this sacred ministry of soul tending, the initial selection of directees is a critical teachable moment. The structural challenges implicit in multiple/dual relationships need conscious tending and the active support of the extended community of accountability in co-discernment through supervision and peer support. This approach brings some consciousness to the decision making in an arena where unconsciousness is what most often causes mischief. While not fail-safe, it does allow for both structure and permeability so that the Spirit can breathe through this holy work with some freedom.

For Further Reflection

1. How does acknowledgement of layers of relationship within the context of a community guide the practice of setting boundaries in the directee/director relationship?

2. What are some structural issues that might occur in the direction relationship? Give examples you are familiar with, if possible.

3. How would you describe a "dual relationship"?

4. What is the responsibility of the director in terms of setting the direction relationship?

 Resources

Greenspan, Miriam. "Out of Bounds." *Common Boundary* (July–August 1995).

Hedberg, Thomas, and Betsy Caprio. *A Code of Ethics for Spiritual Directors.* Pecos, N.Mex.: Dove Publications, 1992.

Heyward, Carter. *When Boundaries Betray Us: Beyond Illusions of What is Ethical in Therapy and Life.* San Francisco: HarperSanFrancisco, 1993.

Keegan, James, SJ. "To Bring All things Together." *Presence* 1, no. 1 (1995).

Lebacqz, Karen, and Joseph Driskill. *Ethics and Spiritual Care.* Nashville: Abingdon Press, 2000.

Lommasson Pickens, Sandra. "Looking at Dual/Multiple Relationships: Danger or Opportunity?" *Presence* 2, no. 2 (1996).

Ragsdale, Katherine Hancock, ed. *Boundary Wars: Intimacy and Distance in Healing Relationships.* Cleveland: Pilgrim Press, 1996.

Silver, Anne Winchell. *Trustworthy Connections: Interpersonal Issues in Spiritual Direction.* Cambridge, Mass.: Cowley Publications, 2004.

From Compassionate Listening to Compassionate Justice
A Call for New Standards

I'd like to begin by asking two questions: Are we doing enough, individually and collectively, for our directees? Are we practicing compassionate justice toward our directees the way we practice compassionate listening? Although we've made some progress in these areas, I believe that we have not yet guaranteed our directees justice.

The Historical Setting for Fostering Human Dignity

As spiritual directors, we value the beauty and dignity of every human person, and seek to foster that beauty and dignity in and through the spiritual direction relationship. That awareness also reaches out to the world around us. We've witnessed women and children, in the face of power and prestige, secure new legal rights and protections. We've watched societies move from merely promoting the value of the human person to prohibiting behaviors that violate human dignity, such as oppressive and unsafe labor conditions, inadequate compensation for work, and child abuse. We seek greater justice to protect human dignity and rejoice when various societies reformulate policies and practices that protect and foster that dignity.

In this tradition, "Guidelines for Ethical Conduct in the Spiritual Direction Relationship" were formulated to articulate the rights and responsibilities of those involved in the spiritual direction conversation: the director and the directee. At heart, these guidelines seek to guard human dignity within the direction relationship and foster the good of both director and directee. The guidelines articulate three general areas of responsibility — for directors in relation to themselves, to their directees, and to their colleagues and the greater society. Let's look briefly now at each of these areas.

Responsibilities for Self

The underlying premise of these responsibilities is that we are to act fairly in relation to ourselves. This includes self-care, professional growth and competence, and personal spiritual growth.

Self-care includes meeting our personal needs outside the spiritual direction relationship. Developing good friendships, taking time for family and other significant relationships, caring for physical needs, and entering into therapy when appropriate are all avenues of self-care. Caring well for ourselves ensures that we will be present to our directees in a healthy way. Getting proper rest, for example, keeps our minds alert and keeps us from dozing during a direction session.

Attending to our professional growth and competence includes undertaking academic study in areas such as theology and psychology to enhance our knowledge and skills as directors. If we are just beginning our work as spiritual directors, we undertake appropriate formation to prepare us for our work. More experienced directors take part in ongoing formation, and both new and experienced directors maintain a relationship with a supervisor to ensure that we do not carry our own hidden issues (e.g., concerns regarding compensation) into direction sessions.

Responsibilities toward Directees

No matter what the appearance may seem to be, we directors hold responsibility in the direction relationship because we sit in the position of power, expertise, and service. Yet no matter how nondirective or collegial we want the spiritual direction conversation to be, we remain the servant of the spiritual directee.

We have several responsibilities as directors, including establishing the nature of the working relationship and the conditions for the spiritual direction conversation (such as time, setting, compensation, etc.), maintaining confidentiality, and always respecting the dignity of directees. By acting responsibly, we allow directees to speak about anything without fear of correction, moralizing, or scolding. We also maintain appropriate physical and sexual boundaries with directees, exercising care about touching and other actions that might invade the sacred personal space of those we direct.

The purpose of the spiritual conversation is to attend to our directee's relationship with God. We violate the dignity of directees whenever we focus the conversation on ourselves, consciously or unconsciously gratify our own needs in and through the conversation, or attempt to coerce or manipulate directees to emulate us.

A young director makes an erroneous assumption concerning something the directee communicates. An experienced director listens from his or her own perspective rather than from the perspective of the directee. Something the directee says triggers something in the director's life and leads the director to miss what the directee is communicating. A director, eager to "be with a directee as a companion," shares something of her own experience to help a directee during a difficult time. These may seem to be little, perhaps insignificant, events. But they are moments when the directee and the director are not in union, when the director has left the directee because of physical tiredness, a personal wound, a desire to help, or other personal needs.

Responsibilities toward Colleagues and Society

We have a responsibility to others because we don't function in isolation but in society. This means that we and our directees are connected to a culture, to communities of faith, to other colleagues with particular expertise, and to systems of governance. We will, from time to time, consult others and refer directees to others. Most significantly, we will maintain and develop relationships with other spiritual directors for continued reflection, collegiality, supervision, affirmation, and challenge. These remind us that we are not alone in our work as spiritual directors and that we need others to journey with us.

Importance of Guidelines

The formulation of the guidelines challenges us to practice the art and ministry of spiritual direction with compassionate justice. All of our responsibilities — toward self as spiritual director, toward our directees, and toward colleagues and society — humble us and remind us that we are not above those basic considerations of fairness and justice. At times, we all fall short of those considerations and must face the fact that our actions (or inactions) may have inhibited or even blocked our spiritual journey with our directees.

It's important to remember that the "Guidelines for Ethical Conduct" are just that — guidelines rather than mandates. They offer aspirational hopes rather than definitive norms of behavior. They were written to inspire directors (and directees as well) to attend to certain ethical realities during their spiritual direction conversations.

The body of data gathered from the experience of spiritual directors when these guidelines were written had not yet developed to bring the definitive clarity of accumulated wisdom. More time was needed to gather and assess the experiences of spiritual directors and directees. But at a minimum, the guidelines named and brought to awareness various areas of right conduct in the spiritual direction relationship.

Future Choices on Behalf of Compassionate Justice

We now face issues, however, concerning the ethical conduct of spiritual directors that require our attention both individually and collectively for the sake of compassionate justice. Among them are establishment of minimum standards for spiritual directors and some kind of certification or licensing of spiritual directors.

Minimum Standards

Minimum standards need to be established for spiritual directors. At present, directors can continue to function as directors even if they dismiss the "Guidelines for Ethical Conduct" as a mere "invitation" toward ethical conduct.

We do not have guidelines for justice; we have norms for justice. We now need minimal standards below which it is clear that a spiritual director is acting unjustly. These standards must address issues of confidentiality, sexual abuse and other inappropriate behavior, accountability, community and collegial responsibilities, and other important issues. Mechanisms for reporting and responding to unjust behavior need to be created as well as forums for defending against unfounded accusations. Articulating these minimum standards and developing the appropriate mechanisms to ensure that they are maintained will protect both vulnerable directees and the integrity of the gift of spiritual direction.

Certification or Licensing

Certification or licensing of spiritual directors is needed to ensure that spiritual directors receive basic formation and evaluation. Accreditation standards need to be developed for formation programs.

Currently a variety of formation programs exist, varying in length from a few months to several years. Some evaluate the strengths and weaknesses of prospective directors while others provide no evaluation. Some offer positive or negative assessments about graduating interns while others do not. Those involved in the formation of spiritual directors need to communicate about and collaborate in determining basic criteria for formation programs that move beyond the "invitations" of the "Guidelines for Ethical Conduct."

Thirty years ago only five programs to form spiritual directors existed in North America; today there are hundreds of such programs. Thousands practice the art and ministry of spiritual direction. A body of data among diverse traditions has been developed over these decades concerning appropriate standards for and expectations of formation programs.

Some will maintain that the ministry of spiritual direction is "of God" and therefore cannot, and should not, be certified or licensed. Yet churches, synagogues, and mosques learned long ago that charlatans were eager to use "of God" in order to gain financial and social advantage over the vulnerable. Because these religious institutions sought to protect their vulnerable members, they established processes and procedures for the formation and certification of religious leaders. We as spiritual directors should do no less.

For Further Reflection

1. How would you describe your personal ethical guidelines as a spiritual director?

2. What personal challenges do you bring to the area of self-care as a spiritual director?

3. How does your faith community or your formation program support the "Guidelines for Ethical Conduct" developed by Spiritual Directors International?

4. What particular cultural norm or tradition might affect your behavior as a spiritual director?

Resources

Guidelines for Ethical Conduct in the Spiritual Direction Relationship. Bellevue, Wash.: Spiritual Directors International, *www.sdiworld.org/ index.pl/ethical_guidelines2.html*

EVOLUTION /
MOVING WITH THE SPIRIT

Widening the Tent
Spiritual Practice Across Traditions

Engaging the practice of "holy listening" in a time of deep spiritual movement and awakening, as well as backlash, requires much of the director-companion. Commentators like Karen Armstrong see great similarities between our time and the Axial Age of 700 to 200 BCE, which was pivotal to the spiritual development of humanity: "All over the world, people are finding that in their dramatically transformed circumstances, the old forms of faith no longer work for them: they cannot provide the enlightenment and consolation that human beings seem to need. As a result, men and women are trying to find new ways of being religious; like the reformers and prophets of the Axial Age, they are attempting to build upon the insights of the past in a way that will take human beings forward into the new world they have created for themselves."[104]

The Shifting Spiritual Landscape

As these shifts of spiritual landscape break open old paradigms, it's not surprising that our formation programs would also be affected. Before the 1980s there were a handful of programs forming spiritual directors. These programs were typically Roman Catholic and had clear institutional connections and heritage, as well as a common vocabulary and clarity of focus. By the mid-1990s these programs — and new ones — had expanded to include candidates from the ecumenical church as well as entirely different faith traditions and noninstitutional spiritual paths such as twelve-step

communities.[105] At the same time, spiritual directors found themselves approached by growing numbers of people outside their own
traditions or any tradition, the one commonality being an evident
hunger for something "more." By 1998, the mission statement of
Spiritual Directors International itself had expanded from an explicitly Christian grounding and focus to "tending the holy around the
world and across traditions."

These currents attest to what Diarmuid O'Murchu calls "a [spir-
itual] movement of our time motivated or driven by a creative
evolutionary force over which we humans have little or no control."[106]
Similarly Don Bisson, FMS, speaks of the deep movements of individuation in the human soul, which are not a choice but an urge, and
notes that this urge and its urgency require us as a human family to
go deeper in every venue, including religion, to negotiate the passage at hand.[107] Walking with another in a way that opens to grace
in upheaval requires both courageous humility and grounded dar-
ing. Spiritual direction in a time such as this is not a calling for the
fainthearted!

Our programs need to look seriously at how can we "widen the
tent" because the creative evolutionary spirit which is moving powerfully in human consciousness crosses traditional boundaries. We
need to find ways of honoring other and emerging traditions without
losing the integrity that comes from depth of location in a particular tradition. Shaping the director's gifts toward holding these
tensions within themselves in creative partnership with the Spirit is
an awesome charge, and is the focus of this piece. While study of the
various traditions and guidelines for evoking sacred story across traditions are valid and useful, my concern here is with formation of the
director's person rather than with information for the director's use.

As spiritual directors, we need to be rooted but not rigid and be
capable of discerning authentic movements of Spirit in a realm where
ego can masquerade as enlightenment. Those of us directors called to
work across traditions need to be free enough to sit without agenda in
service of the directee's unfolding relationship with the Holy Mystery.
Conversion in this context is toward living ever more responsively

to the Spirit in all of life, and not about converting from one faith tradition to another. Providing experiences that assist in the development of a guide's self-awareness and capacity to remain grounded, responsive, and discerning within and across traditions is key.

Historically programs have assumed in-depth spiritual formation of candidates within a particular tradition prior to entering preparation for spiritual direction. Yet George Barna speaks of a cultural "pattern that first emerged more than a decade ago in which [people] feel tremendous freedom to construct their own religious perspectives and practices, regardless of traditions and time-honored teachings."[108] Pat Luce and Bob Schmitt in their article "Looking Beyond Our Tradition: An Invitation to Christian Spiritual Directors"[109] discuss three main groupings of directees emerging from the "environment of many traditions" in which they work. My experience suggests these groupings are also true of many applicants to our formation programs.

1. The first group has its religious roots in Christianity* but

   a. wants to draw from other spiritual traditions and

   b. feels let down by Christianity because they have been wounded.

2. The second group has never been a practicing member of a formalized religion but come for guidance/direction for a variety of reasons, including

   a. a crisis such as a terminal illness or serious personal loss, and

   b. a spiritual experience or yearning that draws them on a spiritual journey.

3. The third group is made up of people practicing in one spiritual tradition who come to a director of another tradition, such as a Buddhist going to a Christian spiritual director.

---

*I assume these same sorts of statements could be made of other traditions as well. (SL)

Providing a Framework
for Holding the Polarities

"I'm spiritual but not religious" is a popular refrain today. Nearly one in five Americans currently describe themselves in this way.[110] Owen C. Thomas notes a "sharp distinction between spirituality and religion, a distinction in which religion is denigrated and spirituality honored."[111] While this perception is consistent with Armstrong's statement that old ways of being religious no longer serve effectively, in truth, the two are interdependent and need to be held in dynamic tension with one another. A foundational preparation for director-interns practicing in the swirling currents of our time is the explicit naming of this tension so they can attend these movements in their own souls and in the soul-stories of directees without being swept into a false dualism.

Neither one — religion or spirituality — is a compartment of the other; each reveals and completes the other. Our spirituality, succinctly described by Thomas Hart as the "lived relationship with Mystery,"[112] is simply an expression of being human. Life places everyone in some kind of relationship with the animating fire that is Spirit's gift. That relationship becomes visible in the weaving of life choices, attitudes, and actions.

If our spirituality is the relationship to the sacred fire[113] within ourselves, others, and the world, then religion is the ring of rocks around that sacred fire. As the living container within which our spirituality is shaped, nourished, and challenged, religion's function is to keep the ember fully alight as an essential part of the whole.

A religious tradition has a body of accumulated wisdom through sacred texts, stories, rituals, practices, and disciplines that help people to access and contain the fire as well as to tend it. A tradition gives vocabulary and concepts to name the experience of encounter with the Holy. This allows growth in conscious availability and gives a community within which we might incline toward the Holy with intention and purpose. A spiritual community at its best gives roots and wings, necessary correction and empowering confirmation.

Fr. Bede Griffiths, a Benedictine monk who lived and worked in India, would hold up a hand to illustrate the relationship between spirituality and religion. "The fingers are the religions," he would say, "but they all come together in the palm, their source."[114] Beginning with this image, I typically ask formation program participants to brainstorm the gifts of each aspect before asking them to self-identify their own preferred "home base." I next invite the "spirituality" and "religion" cohorts to name aloud the downside of their own preferred location. Laughter quickly follows resistance as "ah-ha's" emerge that free and heal. Each participant is finally asked to reflect and write about how the two aspects have woven together in his or her own sacred story to support and to limit freedom to engage work across traditions.

Princeton sociologist Robert Wuthnow names the spirituality/religion tension in contemporary American life as a pull between *seeker-oriented spirituality* and *dwelling-oriented spirituality.* He observes, however, the emergence of a creative third way called *practice-oriented spirituality* that includes elements of personal intention, sustained commitment, social embeddedness, moral responsibility, and the interlacing of personal spiritual practice and service.[115] It is different from seeker-oriented spirituality in that it provides a more orderly, disciplined, and focused approach to the Sacred. It is also different from dwelling-oriented spirituality in that the practices are not dependent on provision by the religious institution. Rabbi Howard Addison sees the challenge for directors as being able to both spiritually abide and spiritually visit from "our own rooted yet searching spirituality of practice."[116]

Supporting a Complete Spirituality

Practice-oriented spirituality is not about pick-and-choose spiritual dabbling. The Dalai Lama is one voice among many who cautions that all faith traditions are not the same, and who recognizes that deep, life-changing understanding of a path is not possible without walking it for significant time.[117] In *After Heaven* Wuthnow comments that the role of leaders today is to live the practice serving as "models of spirituality, rather than guardians or shopkeepers."[118] We need to model what we hope to impart in our programs.

For me, this implies that both the program and the people entering it need to have clearly articulated grounding in a particular wisdom tradition that gives access to what Thomas Hart calls a "complete spirituality." A complete spirituality is more than an amalgam of practice. It has a master story, a theological integrity, and a community of practice that gives an "orientation in life, a set of values to live by, a sense of direction, and a basis for hope, a relationship with Mystery, and a challenge to personal transformation."[119]

That last point is especially important. A primary assumption is that growth in spiritual life requires the sort of wrestling provoked and supported by a particularity of theological commitment and community. From this rooted depth, it is possible to become authentically wide and welcoming, to discerningly incorporate other perspectives and practices, and to work with those of other traditions in a manner truly open to Spirit. In the words of Bede Griffiths, "Our aim is the deepening of our own faith which then becomes more open to others. This is not easy for each [tradition] has its own position. If you try and mix them, taking a bit of Hinduism or Buddhism and adding Christianity, that is syncretism. But if you go deeply into any one tradition you converge on the centre, and there you see how we all come forth from a common root."[120]

Going deep to go broad is structured into the formation program in which I teach from the application and interview process through the selection of program materials. We ask specifically for the longevity of a candidate's religious connection and history as well as for letters of recommendation from those in their spiritual community who see evidence of their personal growth and gifts. This requirement assists us in discerning between two kinds of "homelessness" present in spiritual culture today.

Spiritual Homelessness

Growing numbers of applicants come seeking basic spiritual formation and community because they have been journeying on their own. Often winsome, attractive spirits, there is a rootlessness that Don Bisson relates to the "puer" or "eternal child" archetype embedded in the American spiritual shadow.[121] The primary spiritual task of the puer/puella is to ground, commit, take responsibility, welcome challenge, and encounter limits. To grow up, one must grow down. For this reason, we ask these folks to locate first in a tradition and community as well as in a significant experience of receiving spiritual direction before reapplying.

There is, however, a second kind of homelessness that indicates ripeness for the work of "next step formation" and potential capacity for traveling with others into the depths that cross traditional boundaries. These applicants have wrestled so deeply within their own faith tradition, including with its shadow and their own wounding, that they have opened to the "deep universal" beyond tradition. They typically find their experience of God expanded and enriched by contact with and study of other paths, an openness that can place one painfully on the edge of one's own tradition and community. Conscious attention to the gift and grief of one's personal story within the temporary community of the program is vital. Healing the wounds of tradition frees interior space for the work of awakening to the Spirit's presence in others' stories regardless of the path engaged.

Awakening through conscious entry into the fiery struggles of transformation is what leads Claude d'Estree, a Buddhist *lopan,* to say 90 percent of people need to locate within their own tradition.[122] Like Gandhi — who reportedly said that if we need to leave our own religion to find the truth, we haven't discovered the truth of our own religion — d'Estree encourages directees to explore whether they can find in their own faith what they feel they want from another. He is particularly interested in opening the places of disconnect, pain, and anger for evidence of the Sacred, believing that "Even if they choose a Buddhist path, their anger at their birth religion will rot their Buddhism if it's left unresolved."[123]

This sort of conscious engagement led one teacher connected to our program to recognize how the fight to distance from his birth religion was affecting his freedom to be present to the Spirit's movements in himself and others: "What would it be like to hold my historical tradition with the same sort of contemplative reverence with which I hold a directee?" he wondered aloud one day. His maturing spirit had long ago led him into the deeper waters of transformation through the "scandal" of a particular tradition. Having discovered the wide underground river beneath the wellhead, he was now returning in surprise with new eyes to the place from which he had begun. Surprise — and openness to it — is a hallmark of the Spirit and a marker of what we seek to grow in staff and students alike for freedom to be in service to the Mystery.

Robert Mulholland reminds us that "genuine experience with God is always a decentering experience. The God whom we thought we knew and understood, the God who had become the maintainer and sustainer of our status quo, the God with whom we had become comfortable, this idol we called "God" is suddenly eclipsed by the troubling, disturbing, uncontrolled God who decenters our life by coming to us from the margins and beyond to call us to an often unimagined center where we experience new dimensions of life."[124]

❀ For Further Reflection

1. How does your grounding and community open you to work with people of different traditions, no tradition, or of the margin?

2. How does your tradition/community limit you? Give concrete examples, particularly with directees, if possible.

3. How free are you to engage this sort of work across traditions or "at the edges?"

4. Is there anyone with whom it would be wise for you not to work?

❀ Resources

Addison, Howard. *Show Me Your Way: The Complete Guide to Exploring Interfaith Spiritual Direction.* Woodstock, Vt.: Skylight Paths Publishing, 2000.

Armstrong, Karen. *The Battle for God.* New York: Ballantine Publishing Group, 2000.

Dalai Lama. *The Good Heart: A Buddhist Perspective on the Teachings of Jesus.* Boston: Wisdom Publications, 1996.

Fuller, Robert C. *Spiritual, but Not Religious.* Oxford: Oxford University Press, 2001.

Griffiths, Bede. *The New Creation in Christ.* London: Darton, Longman and Todd, 1992.

Hart, Thomas. *Spiritual Quest: A Guide to the Changing Landscape.* Mahwah, N.J.: Paulist Press, 1999.

Hill, P. C., and K. I. Pargament. "Advances in the Conceptualization and Measurement of Religion and Spirituality: Implications for Physical and Mental Health Research." *American Psychologist* 58, no. 1 (2003): 64–74.

James, William. *The Varieties of Religious Experience.* New York: Random House, 1902.

Luce, Pat, and Bob Schmitt. "Looking beyond Our Tradition: An Invitation to Christian Spiritual Directors." *Presence: An International Journal of Spiritual Direction* 2, no. 3 (1996).

Mabry, John. "Three Modes of Interfaith Direction." *Presence* 10, no. 2 (2004).

Mulholland, Robert M. "Life at the Center — Life at the Edge." *Weavings* (July–August 1998).

O'Murchu, Diarmuid. *Reclaiming Spirituality.* New York: Crossroad, 1997.

———. *Religion in Exile: A Spiritual Homecoming.* New York: Crossroad, 2000.

Skylight Paths, eds. *Who Is My God? An Innovative Guide to Finding Your Spiritual Identity.* Woodstock, Vt.: Skylight Paths Publishing, 2000.

Thomas, Owen C. "Political Spirituality: Oxymoron or Redundancy?" *Journal of Religion and Society.* http://moses.creighton.edu/JRS/2001/ *2001-3.html.*

Wuthnow, Robert. *After Heaven: Spirituality in America since the 1950s.* Berkeley and Los Angeles: University of California Press, 1998.

Zinnbauer, B. J., K. I. Pargament, B. Cole, M. S. Rye, E. M. Butter, T. G. Belavich, et al., "Religion and Spirituality: Unfuzzying the Fuzzy." *Journal for the Scientific Study of Religion* 36, no. 4 (December 1997): 549–64.

Tending the Least of These
Formation for the Margins

Since the Mystery of God is fully present and active in all human experience, the experiences of those on the margins of our society are also filled with the experience of God.

Actually, God is screaming from the edges! It is we who are always shocked at God breaking into our limited vision. Therefore, the evolution and sensitivity to the training of directors towards the poor, the neglected, and those cut off from religious and social institutions has been gradual.

We wish to stir within our interns the discernment of a call to the poor and neglected. Are they willing and able to leave their comfort zones? Are they presently with those on the margins? Are they feeling the stirrings of the Spirit for those on the fringes of our society?

I have over the years continued to network on this topic, especially with Sr. Mary Ann Clifford, RSM who has multicultural experiences, having served in Peru for a long period of time. Her commitment to the poor and to the Hispanic community has led to the formation of Spanish-speaking directors in the Mission district of San Francisco. Mary Ann also brings her multicultural knowledge and sensitivity to formation programs elsewhere.

Over the last few years in New York, I have cosponsored a program with Sr. Kathleen Donnelly, OSU. Our explicit and conscious choice was to support directors to go to those who were not being served by spiritual direction. Our graduates now minister in men's and women's prisons, soup kitchens, hospice programs, shelters, and to cancer survivors, recovering drug addicts, and the housebound. They provide this important and holy ministry to those with few resources. One large group of people I am particularly concerned about is the working poor in rural areas who are struggling with essentials. They have no medical or retirement protection and live with a sense of desperation. God struggles to be heard in all these places, and we are called to bring hope and consolation to them. I feel committed to this process and have been training in this area for years. I therefore would like to share some key elements in the formation of directors for working with people on the margins.

Discernment of Call

An important area in formation programs for spiritual direction is the issue of discernment. This ministry is not merely for good-intentioned people, building skills for professional development. At the heart of spiritual direction is the question of charism: Is this person called to this ministry? Does this formation program assist in confirming, supporting, and enhancing the charism given by God? Supervisors may assist the discernment process through honest feedback and questioning the gifts of individual interns.

I believe the call to the margins is a call within this vocational discernment process. Part of the discernment may involve answering these questions: Who am I being called to serve? Do I desire to move into new directions? Am I being pushed by the Spirit? Do I feel both resistance and attraction toward the marginalized? I believe it is the ethical duty of the training personnel to assist in this ongoing process of being opened by the Spirit to examine these questions. Periods of prayer, input on discernment, days of recollection, and feedback from staff and peers all can help interns (and experienced directors as well) recognize the call to those on the margins.

Experiential Formation

We need to affirm eliminate a "we" vs. "them" mentality when we refer to the margins. Otherwise we immediately isolate ourselves from the power of compassion, empathy, and identification. We are not bringing God to them; rather, we see ourselves as witnesses to the enormous power of God's epiphany in the experiences of brokenness and vulnerability.

Our formation program emphasizes our own reflection on being marginalized and poor in our faith history. By providing reflection time, dyad conversations, and a group sharing experience on the topic of our marginalization, many powerful stories of struggle and God's fidelity emerge. We all carry many secret places of wound and shame. Speaking our experiences of being abused, coming from an alcoholic family, struggling with financial insecurity, immigrant experiences, sexual orientation issues, all of these reflect the holiness of stories and the power of God in our midst. In these sessions, we allow the holiness of the moment to be felt and reflected upon by journaling, poetry, or some other kind of creative expression.

It is important at this point for the interns not to remain overly focused on their own marginalization. I have found that this experiential, personal dimension is not only powerful but also seductive in that it invites interns to become too self-orientated. Though many of us have had marginalizing experiences, few of us in training programs are actually on the margins. We are educated, professional, and mainstreamed. It is important to assist people to look beyond themselves to those less fortunate or who remain in a permanent underclass. It is a challenge to move people beyond themselves to the larger world. This work is not only about self-care, but also care of the world soul. We affirm personal experience, which moves us into the larger world of compassion.

Added Formational Components

Besides the normal formational elements of prayer, religious experience, discernment, and listening skills, I believe that the ongoing formation of spiritual directors needs to include an array of unique topics and processes.

First, in order to go to our own inner margins and to be empowered to go to the outer margins, we need to do shadow work. In Jungian terms, the personal shadow is the forgotten, repressed, unknown, and denied aspect of myself. It is all that we do not want to be which the persona has hidden from our consciousness. To go to the margins is to make the invisible visible and to dialogue with our fearful and rejected parts of self and society. From a Jungian perceptive, shadow work releases repressed energy and is essential for transformation. Shadow work is tough; it challenges our preconceived static images of ourselves and moves us into unknown, dark, and scary places. It is also redemptive; we need to befriend the inner leper. Dream work, active imagination, and journaling are all tools for shadow work. To go to the margins is to confront the collective shadow of our society and religion. It blurs the safe distinctions between good and bad. We are often confronted by society's lies and addictions that support the structures of marginalization and resist change. We rarely speak of evil in training programs, but if we go to those most spiritually vulnerable, we will encounter its reality. Robert Moore's book on evil, *Facing the Dragon,* is written from a Jungian viewpoint and is very insightful. If we deny the reality of evil, we become seduced by a false innocence. This is dangerous. The territory of the shadow must be pursued with caution, trust in God, and the wisdom of both psychology and spiritual practices.

Second, our personal reflection on being marginalized can help us to become a "wounded healer." This is a deep, profound pattern in the human psyche, rooted in ancient shamanism. As part of the training program, the intern needs to become aware of this call to be a wounded healer, a spiritual presence among the broken and the poor. Robert Moore and Douglas Gillette's book *The Magician Within* helps to name the characteristics of the archetype, the methods of accessing the power within it, and the dangers from its shadow elements. Henri Nouwen's classic *The Wounded Healer* helps us to see the contemplative dimension of contemporary ministry. It is important to know this material on both a cerebral level of understanding and a deeper knowing of call and mission. This deeper knowing releases both energy and passion and makes healing available for others. The transformation of consciousness from touching into this archetypal dimension can be life changing.

Third, the formation of directors for the margins demands an education in compassion. This comes primarily from a feeling, not a thinking position. It is important to know the difference between compassion and controlling codependency or human empathy when stories are similar. Compassion is a spiritual virtue gained from personal prayer, surrender, self-forgiveness, and maturity. In Jungian language, compassion is an experience of the deep Self and not of the ego. Receiving compassion from a power greater than ourselves opens us. Having surrendered ego fears, compassion is a gift of the Spirit bestowed upon a wounded soul, transformed by the gratuitous love of the Other. Compassion can then flow through us to another person; we become conduits of God's presence. Humility is at the heart of compassion. When journeying on the margins, compassion becomes the essential presence of being-to-being relationship, deeper than that which might separate us. Only a maturing spiritual life can provide this nonjudgmental, truthful presence to another soul.

Fourth, someone who becomes initiated more fully into life by journeying near the margins may need to do some social analysis. We need to do the hard work of becoming critical lovers of our communities and organizations. This does not mean becoming a social worker or community organizer, but it does mean being a spiritual director who is willing to truly see, hear, and feel the reality of others. It is a subtle call to the prophetic edge. As an example, I have many rural directees who are defined as the "working poor." Though they put in many hours of hard work, they are always nearly in debt, cannot save for the future, and have no medical and psychological care. They are at risk to many tensions and anxieties. Eventually I've had to become more familiar with clinics and systems available for these people. I have joined organizations to change our immoral system, which excludes our citizens from basic dignity as the rich receive enormous tax cuts. I did seek this knowledge. It came to me directly through those affected by injustice. I cannot remain secure with my health care without seeking it for all.

Finally, there is a need for multicultural education and awareness. *Common Journey, Different Paths,* edited by Susan Rakoczy, provides helpful essays in the area of cross-cultural issues in spiritual direction. Exposure to people of other ethnic backgrounds is really the only way to learn that we are not alone in how we experience life and God. Deep listening is most essential on the spiritual journey.

Supervision Issues

Besides the normal issues of supervision, we face particular challenges when we go to the margins. When confronting the shadow both within and without, we may feel the powerlessness and rage in becoming so dependent on God. Our dark emotions may be stirred into recognition for further integration, which can become an opportunity for growth. Resentment stirs when we are not in control. Can we bring our fears and obstacles to the supervisor for assistance? As supervisors, we need to be alert to the unique circumstances of doing this ministry with those on the margins.

We may also have conscious and unconscious guilt in having so much more than others. We need to grow more honest, beyond neurotic guilt and shame. In being more privileged than so many others, we need to work toward justice for all and gratitude for what we have in our lives. Supervision examines the blockages to our self-freedom and openness to the story of the directee with God. Working on the margins is demanding and stressful, and signs of burnout need to be recognized for the health of the director.

In conclusion, training directors for the margins is an invitation to personal and societal transformation. It is a costly but incredibly rewarding experience. God is present in human struggle and seeks recognition no matter the place. God as paradox is found on the edges, disturbing our images of reality and birthing us into the mystery of the Unknowable.

 For Further Reflection

1. Can you recall a time or event in which you were marginalized? What was that experience like? Describe and explore.

2. How can this experience be of service to you as you become a spiritual director?

3. Who are you being called to serve as a spiritual director?

4. How would you describe your resistance and attraction to working with marginalized groups or individuals? What challenges come to mind?

 Resources

Bisson, Donald. "Tending the Holy in the Inner City." *Presence* 1 (January 1995): 34–40.

Coffey, Kathy. *Dancing in the Margins.* New York: Crossroad, 1999.

Dyckman, Kathleen, and Patrick Carrol. *Inviting the Mystic, Supporting the Prophet.* Mahwah, N.J.: Paulist Press, 1981.

Goldstein, Niles Elliot. *God at the Edge: Searching for the Divine in Uncomfortable and Unexpected Places.* New York: Bell Tower, 2000.

Kennedy, Stanislaus, ed. *Spiritual Journeys: An Anthology of Writings by People Living and Working with Those on the Margins.* Dublin: Veritas Books, 1997.

Moore, Robert. *Facing the Dragon: Confronting Personal and Spiritual Grandiosity.* Wilmette, Ill.: Chiron Publications, 2003.

Moore, Robert, and Douglas Gillette. *The Magician Within.* New York: William Morrow, 1993.

Nouwen, Henri J. M. *The Wounded Healer: Ministry in Contemporary Society.* Garden City, N.Y.: Doubleday, 1972.

Rakoczy, Susan, ed. *Common Journey, Different Paths: Spiritual Direction in Cross-Cultural Perspective.* Maryknoll, N.Y.: Orbis Books, 1992.

Vest, Norvene, ed. *Tending the Holy: Spiritual Direction across Traditions.* Harrisburg, Pa.: Morehouse Publications, 2003.

———. *Still Listening: New Horizons in Spiritual Direction.* Harrisburg, Pa.: Morehouse Publications, 2000.

Yancey, Philip. *Soul Survivor: How My Faith Survived the Church.* New York: Doubleday, 2001.

Zweig, Connie, and Jeremiah Abrams. *Meeting the Shadow: The Hidden Power of the Dark Side of Human Nature.* New York: Tarcher/The Penguin Group, 1991.

Cultivating a New Generation
Formation of Future Spiritual Directors

For the last eight years I have been engaged with young adults — all in their twenties and early thirties — in their spiritual journey: interviewing prospective directees, pairing directors with directees, directing, supervising, forming intern spiritual directors. This fall I interviewed forty-one young adults in order to place them with one of twelve intern young adult directors.

I have learned that companioning young adults in the spiritual direction conversation and forming young adults as spiritual directors means dealing with young adult issues and their particular culture. This learning has differed from most of my long-term experience of directing and forming spiritual directors who represent my own age and culture, usually people born before 1970.

In this essay I focus first on young adults as spiritual directees and then on young adults as intern spiritual directors. I offer generalizations, with the realization that each person is an utterly unique individual.

Who Are They?

Generational experts call them "latch-key kids," children of parents whose divorce rates were high and who often pursued idealistic civic causes or fast-track jobs at the expense of traditional home environments. These young adults grew up having to fend for themselves from an early age and are a generation of practical "survivors" whose attitudes are reflected in their values, attitudes, and preferences. They have learned not to rely on much of anything.

179

As many young adults look out on the world, they look with cynical, ironic, sarcastic eyes. One young adult put it this way: "We have inherited the benefits (and leftover baggage) of the civil rights, women's rights, and conservation movements, and we are the first generation to be told that we will not be as financially secure or successful as our parents. The list of economic, social and environmental challenges facing our generation of leaders is long, and I believe this has had a sobering effect on us and our attitudes toward governance, democracy and life in general."[125]

These experiences have also had a profound effect on attitudes about the spiritual of life. One writer commented, "As a result of these kinds of experiences, many young adults have a hard time committing to any specific life project, especially a relationship with another person or with God."[126]

They are skeptics. As one thirty-two-year-old Jesuit intern spiritual director said: "Skepticism is where I feel at home." Webster defines a skeptic as "a person who habitually doubts, questions, or suspends judgment upon matters generally accepted." While they seek closeness with God, they also tend to practice the "hermeneutics of suspicion" given the life-world they have inherited. Because of their age and their culture, they bring specific issues unique to their generation.

Those who write about young adult spirituality find some central themes.

Tom Beaudoin, in the classic *Virtual Faith,* cites four central themes in young adult spirituality: institutions are suspect, ambiguity is central to faith, suffering has a religious dimension, and experience is key.[127]

Issues in Spiritual Direction

Several issues recur in the spiritual direction of young adults, perhaps because of their age, perhaps because of their culture. Let's look at some of the key issues now.

Penchant for Social Justice and Social Concern

Of the several young adults I companion in spiritual direction, I find a great diversity intellectually, politically, economically, psychologically, and socially. But universally they have a hunger for social justice. Many of them volunteer in a soup kitchen, or find some other way to connect with the poor. They see the injustice in the world and are eager to work for justice and peace. Many learn that "faith doing justice" differs from an "idealism doing justice." For them spirituality involves fostering the dignity of those at the margins whom God loves preferentially. I am edified by the awareness, the anguish, and the courageous determination in some young adults at the plight of those at the margins.

Spiritual directors learn that concern about injustices and indignities that burden the poor are central to the vitality of young adults' spiritual journey. Young-adult spiritual directors find great union of spirits with their directees who are eager to serve the poor. Many choose hands-on contact with the poor as they live their spiritual lives. These young adults do not seem to be able to compartmentalize their spiritual living from connecting with those impoverished at the margins.

The Elusiveness of Intimacy and Commitment

Although almost all who are single want a relationship with a significant other, a satisfying relationship does not come easily. They long for closeness and consistency, for someone who is special, but they struggle in finding that special someone. They also struggle over closeness and consistency with God.

Commitment is an elusive reality. David Nantais notes: "If young adults do not acknowledge that there are persons and institutions worthy of their commitments, then they will hop from one superficial relationship or spirituality to another, and they will be left feeling empty and helpless."[128]

Many directees make the initial commitment to see a spiritual director monthly but more than a quarter stop coming in the course of the year, sometimes returning three, six, or nine months later with deep apologies and renewed interest. One directee said, "I continuously set aside relationships because my personal goals are more important than my relationships."

Young-adult spiritual directors recognize that young-adult directees who are reluctant to commit to a life that includes prayerful awareness often carry issues of low self-esteem and identification of one's self with status, productivity, and wealth. Activity, achievement, affluence, and acclamation by others dominate their awareness. Their behavior may mask past hurts and losses. After all, they learned how to survive alone as kids.

Directors help young-adult directees face whatever is being denied. The "hermeneutics of suspicion" holds ignored losses and hurts of the past. Young adults have suspended judgment, and have become skeptical of any process. The independence of surviving on their own easily becomes a way of life, separate from their interiority. In spiritual direction, a growing interior awareness becomes a beacon of light and hope against the cynic. Doubting Thomas becomes a believing disciple. Losses, hurts, doubts, and fears now can become a doorway instead of a dead end. Directors help these young adult directees to recognize and move with those realities that foster greater intimacy with and commitment to self, God, and others.

Spirituality in Movies, Music, and Cyberspace

Many young adults have had little religious education. But contemporary culture does educate them about spirituality and about God. Movies, songs, videos, MTV, commercials — all present and often misrepresent some sense of spirituality, some images of the Divine. Films like *The Matrix* and *Matrix Reloaded* evoke spiritual sensibilities using graphics, concepts, and perspectives with which young adults are comfortable. Many of these experiences are at least a doorway to an experience of the Divine; many are not.

Given this reality, the sifting of discernment is central. Young-adult spiritual directors learn to take these spiritual images from the culture when they speak about spiritual experiences, even though these images are not traditional and are often dismissed by older spiritual directors like myself. These directors, themselves young adults, have been sifting the young-adult culture in search of where it fosters life and where it fosters death unto death. They are ready companions for other young adults in this discernment process. They intertwine the culture and the spiritual journey for other young adults in a way that I, as an older spiritual director, do not.

A World of Growing Fundamentalism

Many young-adult spiritual seekers want a spirituality that is tolerant but has concern for right behavior. They are unhappy about a tolerance that permits anything and everything. Most of them seek values that are universally good and norms that name evil as wrong. And they want something communal, something that holds a tradition.

Some forms of fundamentalism offer the certainty and control young adults seek. People of the previous generation learned to overcome the narrowness of the law and its isolation with the revolution of the 1960s; they broke beyond the practice of the law into nonconventional or postconventional ways of living their spiritual life. Many young adults who are spiritual seekers react to that widespread acceptance of everything. Even though they are ambivalent about many particulars in any religious tradition, they want to know the traditions and be able to pick and choose the traditional religious values that appeal to them.

A few choose to follow the older traditions; some of these succumb to black-and-white answers. Others wrestle with biblical laws and church teachings rather than accept them outright. Though they grapple with these precepts and commandments, they want to know what those laws, beliefs, and practices are. But most do not know the Bible or church wisdom.

Young-adult spiritual directors give these directees time to explore various traditions, time to learn the assets and the limits of what religious laws can offer. Young-adult spiritual directors are often better companions of young adult spiritual journeyers than are older spiritual directors. The older directors have a life history of moving beyond conventional spiritual practices; sometimes their history limits their freedom to allow a spiritual directee to explore practices that seem conformist. To many older spiritual directors, this direction seems regressive.

Struggles with Interiority

Young adults want spiritual experience, but their peers and the culture do not offer them a model. They are focused on doing. They are pressured to succeed in their work; they tend to overwork. The single ones are focused on finding a spouse, getting a promotion, staying in physical shape. Many of the married ones are raising families and holding a full-time job. All of them find it difficult to take time to be still and listen interiorly. They trust experience, but find themselves moving from one experience to another with little reflection on the significance of their experience. They have the experience but miss the meaning.

Young-adult spiritual directors encourage their directees to take a few minutes at the end of the day, make an examen of awareness, notice where life and consolation and centeredness is flowing in their lives as it is, and rejoice in the gift quality of life. Young adults labor to develop eyes and ears of faith to notice and listen to the Mystery present in each moment.

Stillness as Countercultural

Since they were children, these young adults have lived with many comings and goings: school, athletic practice, music lessons, games, and programs. They grew up with a full schedule of activities. Most do not know how to slow down, be still, and listen.

To ask them to remain with a satisfying experience, to relive it, to savor it and see if it holds more is to ask them to act against the way they have been taught. Faithful presence has not been fostered because the "staying with" by government leaders, church ministers, and even parents often has not occurred. Most of these young adults grew up with both parents working; many have parents who divorced.

Early on they learned the suffering of loneliness and abandonment. They have not learned to "stay with" but rather to "survive."

Young-adult spiritual directors patiently and persistently assist their young-adult directees to savor their experience, to attend to the joy and the sorrow of their experience. They invite young-adult directees to be still and live in the present moment, especially in those "waiting moments": in the car at a stoplight or in a traffic jam, in line at a grocery checkout counter, or even in the solitude of something like a weekend retreat.

"Come to the Quiet," a weekend directed retreat, draws young adults into the quiet of contemplative listening. During the weekend retreat, young-adult spiritual directees pray and meet three or four times one-on-one with young-adult directors. In the quiet, as they stay with their experience, they learn the joy of honoring their deeper selves; they become energized, centered. They learn how to be. These young adults learn how to pray in ways that foster centeredness. When they are in the quiet, they savor it and want more. They taste the moment and savor it — now.

Suffering as Meaningful

Losses, failures, anxieties about the future, guilt about the past, and physical and mental pain often lead young adults to search for meaning. Many young adults who seek a deeper spirituality perceive that their peers are in denial of personal suffering or are narcotizing pain in unhealthy ways. These young adults take the force of their suffering and seek to discover something of the Mystery of God in and through their affliction and distress. Their spiritual directors assist them as midwives to treat their distress as an opportunity for personal spiritual growth and depth, attending to the anguish with patience, persistence, and promise.

Issues in Forming Spiritual Directors

Particular issues present themselves in the formation of young-adult spiritual directors. Let's look at some of these issues now.

High Spiritual Learning Curve

Many intern directors are young in life experience but even younger in living a spiritual life, in recognizing spiritual experience. Most have been living a spiritual life with growing awareness for at least four years. Now they are accompanying their peers or those five to ten years younger. They learn quickly in the internship.

Many note how the internship not only helps them in companioning others but in their own spiritual journeys. They find it helpful during internship sessions to experience different forms of prayer. They learn from one another how differently each person prays. They receive peer-group supervision as they present a verbatim of a spiritual direction session. This process fosters noticing their own interior movements with a directee and how each spiritual director responds differently to directees. And yet they notice the common desire with their directees for more, for union with the Divine. They learn to pray for and with their directee. Many directors who are young adults speak of their experience of accompaniment of directees as a most satisfying experience, touching something at the core of their lives. And they often say that accompaniment of others in spiritual direction and retreats helps them in making their own spiritual journey.

Confidence and Competence

Self-assurance and expertise are issues for any intern spiritual director. Young interns may be more brash and less sober because of their limited life experience.

Some tend to err on the side of "I can do this" rather than being contemplative. As one young-adult director said while processing a verbatim of a spiritual direction, "Well, I thought it was time to cut to the chase and move. That is why I said what I said." Of course, the directee noticed this and replied: "Good job. Good insight." Unfortunately this director had left the spiritual directee's soul behind as he "cut to the chase." He offered a helpful insight, more as a pastoral counselor than as a spiritual director.

Other directors are too hesitant, erring on the side of passivity. They are reluctant to assist a directee in reflecting on their experience. These grow as directors in and through their trust of God and of themselves, their willingness to engage the directee more.

With most new young-adult spiritual directors, their own experiences of receiving satisfying spiritual accompaniment has formed them and freed them to be a centered companion with directees. They want to imitate their spiritual directors who have ushered them to their own spiritual growth and development. Their own less satisfying experiences as a directee remind them of behaviors they do not want to repeat. One said: "It is not about me, not about me sharing my own spiritual experiences. A previous director talked too much, especially about herself. I wanted to be listened to as a directee. Now as a director I want to listen." Here they are similar to any intern spiritual director. They find it helpful to notice when their focus moves away from attending to what this directee is seeking and wanting at this moment. Their confidence centers less on technique and more in their own trust of God and the divine Spirit in the moment.

Affective and Effective Spiritual Directors

When they begin an internship, most young adult directors do not know how to be with peers in intimate conversation as spiritual director. Their spiritual directors and mentors have been much older. Now suddenly they are the spiritual director of someone their own age or younger.

Their most common intimate one-on-one experience with peers has been the dating relationship. Moreover, they are alert to the normal sexual attractions that they experienced while dating and which they now feel as they experience the goodness and beauty of a directee in a spiritual direction relationship. They become very aware of the importance of maintaining appropriate boundaries as they claim their power in the spiritual direction conversation. They want to avoid acting out their sexual energy during the spiritual direction conversation, so they tend to pull back their affectivity and run the risk of coming across as cool, aloof, or uncaring. They learn to be a spiritual director who is caring and compassionate, who keeps boundaries and is competent. They learn to pray with their sexual energies contemplatively. They are also learning that they must continue to seek out supervision.

Contemplative Directors

Because they are idealistic, the danger of communicating or even imposing their spiritual ideals upon their directees is high. As they grow in self-acceptance of themselves in their own spiritual journey, they are able to accept directees where they are, with their strengths and weaknesses. Many young-adult spiritual directors move easily to pastoral counseling, eager to be of help, inclined in their care to "fix" the directee, attempting to assist their directee in conquering whatever the difficulty. They find it challenging to wait in the darkness with their directees, patiently and with faith, hoping that the dawn will come.

As young-adult directors become more contemplative in their own lives, they move beyond trying to "help" their directees. They become more attuned to their own journey with its rhythms of light and darkness. They face their own darkness and understand it as a time to believe, trust, and be loving. Similar to older spiritual directors, these young-adult directors learn that if they trust, their young-adult directees will in time find their own rhythms and light in the Mystery.

Even though young adults live in a culture that presents attitudes, beliefs, and values different from those of their elders, many similarities run across the generations. Young and old value spirituality. They want to listen to their spiritual hunger and thirst, and want to experience those yearnings fulfilled. They want intimacy with God, themselves, and others. Spiritual direction offers them an opportunity to be attentive, grow in awareness, and make discerned choices.

Internships for younger spiritual directors foster companionship with younger spiritual journeyers where a contemplative attitude, faith-filled listening, affectively centered responses, and discerned movements become helpful tools in evaluating contemporary pop culture by those who have been shaped by that culture.

For Further Reflection

1. As directors, what risks do we need to take to make ourselves available to the next generation?

2. What personal challenges do you face in choosing to be in spiritual conversations with young adults?

3. What attracts you when you consider the thematic issues brought by young adults to spiritual direction?

4. What gifts do you feel that young adults can offer the ministry of spiritual direction?

Resources

Beaudoin, Tom. *Virtual Faith: The Irreverent Spiritual Quest of Generation X.* San Francisco: Jossey-Bass, 1998.

"Charis Young Adult Ministry," *www.yamchicago.org.*

Hoover, Brett. *Losing Your Religion, Finding Your Faith: Spirituality for Young Adults.* Mahwah, N.J.: Paulist Press, 1998.

Nantais, David. "Whatever Is Not Ignatian Indifference: Ministry to Young Adults." *Studies in the Spirituality of Jesuits* (Fall 2004).

Webster's New World College Dictionary. Springfield, Mass.: Merriam-Webster, 1996

Wensing, Kristen. "A National Conversation on Generational Ethics, Duke University, June 24, 2002." *www.contentofourcharacter.org.*

Journeying Together
The Practice of Group Spiritual Direction

At "The Heart of Spiritual Guidance" conference sponsored by the Institute of Transpersonal Psychology in January 2005, the venerable Rabbi Zalman Schachter-Shalomi stressed the absolute need in our world right now for "ensembles of people" meeting together, forming "webs of consciousness" that are hopeful and healing. The experience of group spiritual direction is certainly this — and more: the coming together of individuals, grounded in a sense of Divine Presence, to share their spiritual lives in a confidential atmosphere of prayerfulness, silence, quiet reflection, and contemplative listening. This is an opportunity for spiritual direction in a small, supportive group context and ambiance of mutuality.

Group Spiritual Direction Program

In response to a sense of the growing need and desire for group spiritual direction opportunities, my colleagues and I began a pioneering new nine-month group spiritual direction internship program for already-trained and experienced directors. The program, described as "spiritual direction for the twenty-first century," was met with tremendous enthusiasm by many directors of different faith traditions. Some of these directors, having participated in and/or facilitated other kinds of groups, had a sense of how valuable spiritual direction might be in a group context; other directors were in situations or geographic areas where the lack of available directors made the group format the only direction opportunity possible for directees. Many directors voiced a clear sense of a "call within a call," a deep attraction to broadening their skills in order to offer spiritual direction with groups.

What draws spiritual directors to this program is its spiritual rootedness as well as its practical and multidimensional approach to growth, learning, and development. Throughout the nine-month internship, the intentional focus of the program is to provide the group spiritual direction intern with:

* Experiences that allow the conscious awareness of the presence and dynamic activity of the Spirit in their individual lives and in the life of the internship group as a small spiritual community
* Experiences of a wide variety of different forms/models of group spiritual direction ranging from the very simple forms with no cross-talk to progressively core complex models
* Adult learning modalities that provide the interns with essential knowledge, understandings, and practical skills necessary for the group spiritual director
* Opportunities to reflect on learnings and experiences in the internship group
* Ongoing practice of self-supervision through feedback, evaluation, and written responses to the group spiritual direction experiences
* Conscious practice and development of group leadership skills essential for the facilitation of group spiritual direction
* Personal awareness of the ways the Spirit may be prompting interns to share themselves, their gifts, their new knowledge, and group direction skills with others.

Program Description and Overview

What follows is an attempt at a succinct description and overview of this group spiritual direction training program.

At the heart of each three-hour session of the nine-month program is an experience of a different model/form of group spiritual direction. As in individual spiritual direction, we understand that

God is the true director present and guiding each group participant as well as the group as a whole. The quality of the sharing of life experiences is prayerful, slow-paced, contemplative, reverential, and confidential. The sharing is dialogic in the literal Greek sense of the word: *dia* — "coming through" and *logos* — "the word, the meaning." We drop pre-fixed agendas and open our consciousness to allow the word, the meaning to come through. This kind of sacred listening and sharing is not a dialogue of ideas, but more a languaging of heart and soul.

There are many distinctive characteristics of group spiritual direction. These include an extended time of silent prayer as a group; a pervasive silence that is the ground from which participants speak and share; the uprooting of narrow, biased, fixed ideas about God and the spiritual life as participants share; an often palpable and amplified felt sense of God present and active in individuals and in the group; an ever-changing, evolutionary growth process throughout the life of the group that requires the group director to practice an adaptive, creative, and experimental approach as the facilitator. At the conclusion of the group direction experience, we emphasize the provision of time for tasting and savoring the experience through silence, journaling and shared reflections; the inclusion of intercessory prayer for the group and for others; and a commitment to ongoing prayer for group members and faithfulness to meeting times.

As interns learn more about the nature of group spiritual direction, a familiar image is used to clarify the essential aspects of the experience. The image is one of a pebble dropped into a still pond with ripples then radiating out from the center. In this image, prayer is the core, the still point of the experience. Sourced in this conscious awareness and communion with God, group participants are in silence and an atmosphere of quiet reflection. It is out of this ground that the sharing and contemplative listening arise. The inclusion of intercessory prayer intentionally links the graces of the group spiritual direction experience with others and the world. Participants in the training program are asked to reflect on and discover other images of the group direction experience that exemplify their own sense of the nature and process of group direction.

Included in each month's training session is a didactic presentation and focused conversation on a wide variety of topics essential for the development of a prayerful, knowledgeable, understanding, and skillful group spiritual directors. The modes of teaching and learning are co-creative and dialogic, honoring the wisdom being shared by all the interns. The themes presented and explored include but are not limited to the nature of group spiritual direction; the similarities and differences between individual spiritual direction and group direction; the distinctive characteristics of group direction; the development of spiritual community; prayer and the contemplative dimension of group direction; a review of the listening skills of the spiritual director; the introduction and development of group leadership and facilitation skills; the responsibilities of the group director; qualities important to cultivate as a group spiritual director; discernment in group direction; the principles of group dynamics and the stages of growth and development of groups; and the importance of ongoing self-supervision, individual supervision, and mentoring for the group director.

Throughout the entire training program, we provide ongoing opportunities for sharing and discussion of any issues, concerns or questions, as well as an "open forum" time for further exploration of topics related to the group direction process.

The Threefold Practicum

An invaluable and very significant aspect of the group spiritual direction training program is the threefold practicum:

First, at each monthly session a different model or form of group direction is presented, explained, and experienced by the whole intern group. Time is given for reflection, journaling, gathering the learnings, feedback, and evaluation. During the second half of the program, there is a dramatic and exciting shift. The interns self-select into three co-facilitation teams. Each team of intern group directors is then responsible for the planning, creation, design, implementation, and co-facilitation of the group spiritual direction experience at the center of one monthly session (usually in February, March, or April). This includes arranging the environment for gathering, including an altar centerpiece, as well as any use of readings, art, music, and symbols, etc., to create an atmosphere of sacred space. Following the group direction experience, the whole group as well as the staff have an opportunity to reflect, gather the learnings, and offer constructive feedback. This entire experience is a creative, multidimensional, and profound learning opportunity for the group direction interns. Often very innovative models of group direction are designed and implemented — true pioneering developments in the art of group spiritual direction. This is very inspiring for the whole group, including the staff.

Second, the interns also individually design and develop a "project-in-process," a group spiritual direction experience or series they plan to offer in the future. As each intern presents a written and detailed description of his or her project, the whole group responds as a "think tank" for the presenter — asking clarifying questions, offering constructive suggestions, and responding to any concerns, issues, or queries the presenter might have. These brainstorming sessions provide invaluable support for the intern group directors as they seek to create and implement truly graced experiences of group spiritual direction for those they serve.

Third, throughout the training program, interns gather resources that may be helpful for them as they ready themselves to offer group direction. These resources most often include a variety of readings such as sacred scriptures, prayer collections, special books, and poetry as well as music, icons, images, photos, symbols, and artwork that contribute to the creation of an atmosphere of prayerfulness. Toward the end of the program, participants share these resources with the whole group. This introduction and inclusion of new and fresh resource materials is very helpful for the interns as well as the staff.

Each month there is an assignment given that includes a written reflection/self-supervision paper as well as required reading.

The reflection/self-supervision paper is a personal response to each month's group spiritual direction experience. As the basis for their self-supervisory response, interns select one or two questions from a comprehensive list of "catalytic questions" they have been given. That list includes these questions:

- Was I aware of the presence and activity of God, the movement of the Spirit in myself? In other individuals? In the group as a whole?

- As a directee and also a co-director, where did my words and silence seem to be coming from? What personal feelings, agendas, filters, biases, and assumptions influenced my way of being and participating in the group spiritual direction experience?

- In the context of affirming this group direction experience as a locus for God's presence and activity in my own life, what am I discovering about relationships, fear, trust, risk, and selflessness as I attend to the dynamics of this group?

Obviously, answering these questions in a written paper requires deepening awareness, reflection time and probing self-supervisory attentiveness on the part of each intern.

Required Reading Component

The required reading component of the group spiritual direction program includes relevant books, articles, handouts, and other resource materials. At the monthly sessions, discussions about these materials focus on what the interns found most valuable as they continue to learn and grow as group spiritual directors. At times, a written reflection on a book is included in the monthly assignment. Some of these readings are listed as resources at the end of this chapter.

Evaluation of Learning and Growth

As the training year draws toward a close, the interns write an evaluation of their learning and growth as a group spiritual director. This harvesting of the graces and fruit of their experiences is a benefit for them as well as the staff who welcome this feedback in planning the following years' programs. Some of the most consistently mentioned fruits of the program include the following:

- A deepening awareness of the often awesome and surprising presence and movement of the Spirit in individuals and in groups
- A much broader sense of the diverse and unique ways each person may experience and language the Divine
- Wider experience of how others pray
- Greater capacity for tolerance, compassion, confidentiality, and spiritual intimacy in a spiritual community
- Maturing growth as a spiritual director with more reliance on the Spirit, gratitude, confidence, and freedom to serve others
- Further development of listening skills and group leadership skills as well as increased facility and suppleness as a group spiritual director
- Awareness and understanding of the progressive stages of group development and dynamics as well as the blessings and challenges inherent in the life of groups
- Graced and practical experience participating in, planning, designing, and implementing a variety of models and forms of group spiritual direction.

As the training year ends, and sometimes even before that, many interns begin to offer and facilitate a variety of group spiritual direction experiences for those they serve. Their joy and enthusiasm for this ministry of group spiritual direction clearly is a gift, a charism for which they are so grateful. These group spiritual directors have learned to "lean back into God" for guidance, inspiration, and confidence.

In our world and social atmosphere today, we face a continuing need and hunger for "ensembles" of hope, joy, and love sourced in God. In response to this need, we continue to offer the group spiritual direction training program and will be adding a five-day residential intensive program in the summer of 2005. We also offer continuing opportunities for long-distance supervision, mentoring, and tutorial assistance via telephone for those in other geographical locales.

How provident of the Spirit to be stirring so many spiritual directors to train for this ministry of group spiritual direction at this time. It is truly a blessing, comfort, and healing for our global family.

 ## For Further Reflection

1. Do you have a sense of a "call within a call" to train as a group spiritual director and serve others through this ministry with groups?

2. Have you participated in or facilitated any groups that have had some of the distinctive characteristics of a group spiritual direction experience?

3. Is there an image of group spiritual direction that comes to mind and heart for you?

4. Are there fruits of the group spiritual direction training program that you might desire for yourself?

Resources

Carnes, Robin Deen, and Sally Craig. *Sacred Circles: A Guide to Creating Your Own Women's Spirituality Group.* San Francisco: HarperSanFrancisco, 1998.

Corey, Gerald. *Theory and Practice of Group Counseling.* Pacific Grove, Calif.: Brooks/Cole, 1995.

Corrigan, Winifred, RC. "Group Spiritual Direction." *New Covenant* 33 (1974): 336–43.

Garfield, Charles, Cindy Spring, and Sedonia Cahill. *Wisdom Circles: A Guide to Self-Discovery and Community Building in Small Groups.* New York: Hyperion, 1998.

Dougherty, Rose Mary, SSND. *Group Spiritual Direction: Community for Discernment.* Mahwah, N.J.: Paulist Press, 1995.

———, ed. *The Lived Experience of Group Spiritual Direction.* Mahwah, N.J.: Paulist Press, 2003.

Edwards, Tilden. *Spiritual Friend: Reclaiming the Gift of Spiritual Direction.* Mahwah, N.J.: Paulist Press, 1980.

Heider, John. *The Tao of Leadership.* Atlanta: Humanics New Age, 1985.

Kline, Ann. "Widening the Lens: The Gift of Group Spiritual Direction." *Presence* 10, no. 2 (June 2004): 38–42.

Lord, Donna, GNSH. "An Experience of Group Spiritual Direction." *Review for Religious* 46, no. 2 (March–April 1987): 279–94.

McKnight, Felicia. "Group Spiritual Direction: Intentionality and Diversity." *Presence* 1, no. 3 (September 1995): 29–44.

Peck, M. Scott, MD. *The Different Drum: Community Making and Peace.* New York: Simon & Schuster, 1987.

Senge, Peter M. *The Fifth Discipline: The Art and Practice of the Learning Organization.* New York: Doubleday, 1990.

Friends of God and Prophets

Transformation for Justice

God has been really concerned about the way the world is heading. There seems to be so much greed and strife and wars and troubles. People are just not taking care of one another. So God resolved to send one of the angels down to earth to check it out. After a few days, the angel came back and reported, "It's even worse than you thought, God. About ninety-five percent of the people are on the wrong path; but the other five percent are really wonderful."

Hmmm, thought God. That sounds really bad. Maybe that angel was exaggerating. I'd better get a second opinion.

So God summoned a second angel and sent her off to see what was going on around the world. A while later she returned, shaking her head. "I regret to inform you, God, but the situation is exactly as the first angel reported: ninety-five percent of the people are not following your ways; they are lost souls. The other five percent, however, are truly wonderful."

God listened and pondered what to do. Finally God decided that the first step should be to send an e-mail to the five percent to encourage them to keep up the good work.

So, do you know what was in that e-mail???

No? I guess you didn't get one either!

Actually, for the past few months, I've been waiting for a direct line myself from God to help me with this essay! That help came in the form of two dear friends in our Mercy community: a biblical theologian, Mary Criscione, whose insights into the scriptural understanding of prophecy form the foundation for what follows, and Marilyn Lacey, whose contemplative listening and questioning

199

distilled what I hope will be a coherent reflection from my many years and experiences as a trainer of spiritual directors. I offer these thoughts as a peer among peers, wanting to begin a conversation among us all on this questions: Where do we see the prophetic edge of spiritual direction?.

I have entitled this chapter "Friends of God and Prophets." You may recognize the phrase as the title of Elizabeth A. Johnson's 1998 book on the communion of saints. However, Elizabeth herself lifted it directly from the Hebrew Scriptures, from Wisdom 7:27, which reads " . . . in every generation, she [wisdom] passes into holy souls, and makes of them friends of God, and prophets."

I want to explore how God's action in our lives first creates friendship, then transforms us to the point where we see the world as God sees it, and how this necessarily moves us, willingly or not, into a prophetic stance with the poor and against the unjust structures of our world. In that context, we can look together at how our training programs encourage or impede this threefold transformation. My personal hunch is that we are far better at training folks to be friends of God than we are at preparing them for the continuing conversion which puts us at odds with a world generally hostile to prophets. I look forward to our dialogue together on that point!

So, let's consider these three phases in our wonder-full, perilous journey into God: First, becoming friends of God. Second, being transformed such that we see things, people, events, indeed, all of creation, from God's perspective; and third, staying with this ongoing conversion, this prophetic stance, as it turns life upside down — or, more precisely, as all hell breaks loose!

Phase One / Becoming Friends of God

Who wouldn't want to be a friend of God? It is the deepest desire of our hearts: to be fully known and accepted, loved as we are, without reservation; wholly held by God's compassion, healed of our brokenness, set free to be our best selves. For some few people I have known, this awareness of being utterly embraced by a loving God has been a priceless gift from their earliest years. For most of us, however, it takes a very long time to absorb the reality of God's love, no longer just in our heads but right down to our fingertips and our toe-tips! The good news is, after all, beyond all that we could ask or imagine. But when it does take hold, and a human person experiences the radical unconditionality of God's love, then miracles do occur: joy surges up, affection and freedom emerge, whole new worlds open up.

In our spiritual direction training programs, I believe we have focused long and well on helping persons to become "friends of God." We explore Scripture to discover who this amazing God is, the One who delights in showing mercy, who desires that we have life and have it abundantly (John 10:10). With our interns, we study psychology, and human growth and development, to understand, yes, that we are wonderfully made (Psalm 139) but also that we are fragile and easily hurt, slow to forgive and to heal or be healed. We examine our theologies, our approaches to making sense of our lives, the elements that shape our spirituality. We teach others how to listen contemplatively, how to identify movements of God, resistance to grace, the tending of the Holy. We need to do all this: as St. Teresa of Ávila famously groaned, "God save me from ignorant directors!" As trainers, I believe we have done our homework in this area, and learned a lot together.

We are privileged witnesses to the inner journeys, the struggles, the insights, the pain, the growth, the conversion of persons who confide in us, who come to us for guidance and companionship along the way. We see people literally becoming "friends of God." This is no small treasure shared with us! If you are like me, you have many moments during or after a spiritual direction session where you are in awe, and deeply humbled, by the action of God in the lives of your interns or directees. How often I have almost been jealous of their intimate experiences of God!

So, I do think that our training programs, our collaborations and regional support structures, our Spiritual Directors International symposia and conferences, and *Presence* magazine have done tremendous good. We are engaged together, more and more, in learning how to help people realize that when God looks at them, God sees their goodness. God's stands at the door of their hearts knocking (Rev. 3:20), wanting only to be allowed in, to sit them down and serve them, to share God's own self with them, to speak with them intimately as a dear friend or even passionately as a lover whose desire will not be held back.

However, I invite us to examine whether our training programs stop at this level; namely, helping individuals to feel good about themselves — a sort of therapy with spiritual trappings — that does not go any further.

Phase Two / Being Transformed

The next phase, which follows upon this growing friendship with God, is what I call being transformed, or "beginning to see life from God's perspective." Friendships change us; intimate relationships all the more so. It should not surprise us, then — though it almost always does — that becoming a friend of God has consequences. Surely it has consequences on the personal level: as God's forgiving, life-giving mercy flows into me, it is meant to flow through me into all of my other relationships. As God's joy fills my heart, I naturally share that "enthusiasm" (*en-theo*) with the people around me. As Dorothee Soelle writes in *The Silent Cry: Mysticism and Resistance,* "Mystical experience is bliss and simultaneously it makes us homeless."[129] We can no longer stay as we were, in our own comfort zones, cherishing the graces received. As God makes it clear that God wants to be the center of our lives, then we have to toss out the old idols that have until now held that space captive, and reevaluate everything in the light of this one absorbing priority. Though it often will be terribly difficult, this is never a grim task, since it is prompted by a love that surges with joy.

This transformation can be quite sudden and radical — the response to an inbreaking of grace as seen, for example, in Mother Teresa or St. Francis. More likely, it will be a slower dawning of what

it means to be a friend of God: over time, values change; relationships are affected; lifestyles shift to align us more with our experience
of God.

Whether sudden or gradual, the mark of authenticity for a developing friendship with God and its consequences in our lives will
always be that the experience is not clung to as a private grace. Again
I quote from Dorothee Soelle: "There is no experience of God that
can be so privatized that it becomes and remains the property of one
owner, the privilege of a person of leisure, the esoteric domain of the
initiated."[130] For those of us born and raised in the United States, the
tendency toward rugged individualism remains deep and stubborn.
We like our God one-on-one, in the privacy of our own hearts. This
"Me-and-God" spirituality (or, in our better moments, God-and-
Me), while quite strong and pervasive in the Western world, does
not describe the God of the Scriptures or the God of Jesus or the
God of the early church or the God of the saints or of other religious
traditions. There we see always that God is forming a people, not a
collection of individuals. God is bringing about community, not sav-
ing souls. God's justice is about right relationships with all creation,
not just setting me right with God.

Thus, when we become a true friend of God, there will be external changes in our life. What really happens when we experience
God is that we glimpse what Quakers call the "unity in the midst of
commotion," the deep, authentic oneness of all beings despite the
dissonance and separateness that appear on the surface. By God's
own action in our lives, we begin to see with God's eyes, hear with
God's ears, speak what we hear from God, do what God does, as we
more and more desire only what God desires. This is precisely what
the prophets experienced: feeling what God feels, then speaking and
acting out of that experience.

So, in our training centers, where we are learning together how to
discern God's action in our human experience, we need to ask: *What
God are we looking for? What God are we training others to pay attention
to?* Is it the God of the politically powerful, dividing the world neatly
into good and evil and wreaking vengeance on one's enemies? Is it the

God of the televangelists, preaching an ethic of success and wealth as proofs of God's approval? Is it the current best-selling, flag-waving, bumper-sticker God of Jebez, whose prayer is that God will "enlarge my territory so that I never come to any harm"?

Or is it the God of the prophets, where we see Hosea describing a God as helpless as a spurned lover, who must go to extraordinary lengths to woo us back into the divine embrace? The God of Jeremiah, whose passion for us wraps itself around us like a loincloth around a man? The God of Zephaniah, who brings about reconciliation and then dances joyfully in our midst? The God of Isaiah, who demands justice for the oppressed, and fair wages for the laborer? The God of Jesus, who warns us not to pattern our lives on the religious professionals who pay tithes and accept place of honor in society, all the while trampling the rights of the poor?

As Abraham Joshua Heschel wrote forty years ago in his superb book *The Prophets,* "The Prophet disdains those for whom God's presence is comfort and security: to [the prophet] it is a challenge, an incessant demand.... The prophet's word is a scream in the night.... God is never neutral, never beyond good and evil. [God] is always partial to justice.... The characteristic of the prophets is not foreknowledge of the future, but insight into the present pathos of God."[131]

In the Hebrew Scriptures, prophecy is distinctive but complex. Prophets were both women and men, both cultic priests and their opponents, in both professional religious roles and in secular occupations, both within the king's circle and critical of it. Some, like Elijah and Elisha, healed. Some, like Miriam, led communal celebrations. Some, like Jeremiah, performed symbolic acts of judgment. Some, like Isaiah and Hosea, wrote. Always, whatever their status, the genuine prophets saw the reality of their day from God's perspective and communicated that perspective to the people, whether it was a message of judgment or of consolation.

In the New Testament, Jesus is depicted as referring to himself as a prophet (Mark 6:4) and as being so understood by others (Mark 8:28, Luke 24:19, Acts 7:37). Like Elijah, Jesus heals and provides food miraculously. Like Amos and Jeremiah, he performs symbolic acts of judgment (Mark 11:15) and castigates the religious establishment of his day (Mark 12, Matt. 23). The communities established in his name include prophets as communal authorities (1 Cor. 12:28, Acts 13:1), as leaders of prayer (1 Cor. 14:39), and as linked with the presence of the Spirit and the need for discernment (1 Thess. 5:19–22).

Throughout all of Scripture, the true prophet sides with the poor. The *false* prophet, on the other hand, bolsters the comfort and security of the powerful. The true prophet points out the divine presence and power, always in the context of community, and with a view toward judgment that moves the people toward justice. The *false* prophet engenders an insular sense of security and inner peace in individuals that does not lead to action.

The links with spiritual direction are clear. Both prophet and spiritual director stand in a position of recognizing and mediating God's perspective, proclaiming God's ways. Both prophet and director stand in (sometimes critical) service of the larger community even while addressing individuals; social responsibility is the prerequisite stance. Both prophet and spiritual director attend to the divine valuation of actions and attitudes, and their consequences for choosing life or death in the eyes of God.

Phase Three / The Social Consequences of Conversion

Dietrich Bonhoeffer called the social consequences of conversion the "cost of discipleship." Authentic grace never comes cheap. Emmanuel Levinas, a twentieth-century Jewish philosopher, puts it simply: "To know God means to know what has to be done." And knowing what has to be done, alas, generally means that one's life will be turned upside down. "Success is not a name of God," says Martin Buber. But don't we love being successful? Wouldn't we all want, at least on a subconscious level, to be known as the best trainer of spiritual directors? To develop the training curriculum recognized worldwide? To have our particular center touted as the model for all

others? But success is not a name of God. Conversion, that movement beyond being a friend of God to becoming a prophet of God,
inevitably sets us apart from and even up against the way most people
see and live and think and feel. It made St. Francis a laughingstock in
his town. It landed John of the Cross in prison in his own community.
It cost Gandhi his life. It pushed Dorothy Day to actions on behalf of
justice that were incomprehensible to most of her contemporaries.
But still, most of us miss the radical consequences of God's presence in our lives. Take the title of Dorothee Soelle's book to which
I've referred already: *The Silent Cry: Mysticism and Resistance.* Be honest, when you hear "resistance" in the context of mysticism, don't
you think of a directee evading, stonewalling, or resisting God? But
Soelle's title actually refers to communal resistance to unjust social
structures — the inevitable consequence of mysticism!

David Lonsdale has an excellent chapter in the recent book
Handbook of Spirituality for Ministers entitled "Spiritual Direction as
Prophetic Ministry." In it, he quotes from Grace Jantzen's *Power,
Gender and Christian Mysticism* on the insidious possibility that involvement in spirituality, which seeks private inner peace, actually
deflects us away from substantive issues of peace and justice in the
real world. The net result, Jantzen writes, "is the reinforcement of
the societal status quo, as intellectual and religious energy is poured
into an exploration of private religiosity rather than into social and
political action for change. And this in turn has the effect not only
of turning the attention of those seeking deepened spirituality away
from issues of justice, but also of leaving the efforts for justice to
those who have abandoned concern with spirituality, seeing it as
having nothing to offer in the work for structural change."[132]

True conversion, on the other hand, always thrusts us into community. And conversion requires contemplation. Without community,
the prophet slips into arrogance. Without contemplation, the prophet
cannot move beyond his or her anger at the world's injustices. If my
words must speak for the powerless, then only God can energize me
with both passion and compassion for the long haul.

So, in our training centers, how do we train for social consciousness? Are we teaching people to tend individual broken hearts without also teaching them to listen to the cries of humanity? Are we teaching compassion for those who need healing, without watching for the divine passion that yearns to change the unjust structures that oppress the poor? I would suggest that we examine our training programs in this light and ask ourselves these questions:

- Are we ensuring that the theologies undergirding our training include this whole notion of prophetic justice? Do our theologies embrace the prophetic edge, or shy away from what may be uncomfortable or challenging?

- Are we globally aware? Are we acting from the conviction that all of life is interconnected? Are we being prompted by God's Spirit to participate in — or even lead — the vast shifts of consciousness that are shaping our world today: the human rights movement, the environmental movement, and others? What would this mean on a practical level for our programs?

- Who is it that we train? In general, our starting point has been mostly first world, mostly white, mostly middle- or upper-middle class. Don Bisson, a spiritual trainer, wonders whether we are guilty of creating "spiritual apartheid" by working with elites who have time, money, and leisure for our training programs. How can we ensure that the circle widens?

- Are we desirous of being countercultural in order to be more attuned to the values and demands of the gospel? Are we even aware of the worldview we inherited?

- Are we connecting our interns to voices that are not mainstream? How culturally diverse are we? How eager to embrace other cultures? How urgently do we seek out the marginalized to learn from them? Surely the Lord hears the cry of the poor. Do we?

Rabindranath Tagore, the Indian poet, tells the story of a wealthy king, a *raj,* who desired to see God. He assembled a tremendous retinue of elephants and carriages and royal attendants, forming a magnificent procession slowly making its way across India, toward the holiest temple. As they passed through village after village, they invited onlookers to join the pilgrimage, and thousands joined the throng. But one old man, desperately poor, stood quietly in front of his hut without moving. "Come on," his neighbors urged, "This is our chance. Let's go visit God." "No," he whispered, "I shall wait for God to visit me." Then they hurled abuse at him: "You? A peasant! Don't be a fool; even the mighty *raj* must travel to see God! What makes you think God would come to visit you?" The man stood his ground and answered, "Who but God would ever visit the poor?"

The best name for God is "SURPRISE," says Benedictine Brother David Stendl-Rast, because God is always doing something new (Isa. 43:19), always moving beyond what we have already known. If this is true, then we are seriously at risk of missing the living God when we set up guidelines and curricula and teach from our carefully crafted notes. God resists packaging; the real God cannot be domesticated.

The disturbing truth here is that what may well have been prophetic thirty years ago, could easily be getting in God's way today. Thirty years ago, spiritual direction was primarily the domain of ordained clergy; it was largely a Catholic phenomenon, and it occurred normally within the sacrament of confession, or some other private setting with a priest. Thirty years ago, it was quite bold to imagine spiritual direction being done by the nonordained — and downright brazen to suggest it could be done by women! Yet that is precisely what God's spirit seemed to have in mind, and so it came to be: a worldwide reality that is now marvelously ecumenical and inclusive of people from all religious traditions. It happened first at the margins, and gradually became accepted, and then in a sense, "popular." Gradually centers were established to teach others how to become directors; curricula were designed. Now we have ethical guidelines and national convenings and even business cards that say "spiritual director." But over time, unless we continue to listen for the prophetic edge, these very structures and programs and codified ways of training spiritual directors might themselves obstruct the living God whose ways can never be structured or codified. The only way to avoid this is to stay engaged daily with the living God whose word, Jeremiah says, "is like fire, like a hammer shattering rock" (23:29).

The only way we can remain faithful to the God who is always surprising us, always moving us toward the poor, always stretching our boundaries, is to become deeply contemplative ourselves, to take, in the words of Walter Burghardt, "a long, loving look at the real."[133]

God is always at work, and nothing we do or fail to do will stop this divine energy. Our task is to pay attention and to nurture the in-breaking of the prophetic among us. This we do by sustained contemplative prayer and by refusing to isolate ourselves from the poor. If we daily risk this contemplative engagement with God, and we regularly choose to leave our comfort zones and move outward toward the marginalized, then in our training programs we will not be seduced by certificates and honors, or even by being invited to speak at an Spiritual Directors International conference. Rather, we will remain attentive to the subversive values of God who identifies with the "least in our midst," the strangers, the outcasts; the God who pulls down the mighty from their thrones and lifts up the lowly. We will be watching for the movement from consolation-that-leaves-us-comfortable, to consolation-that-sets-us-afire-for-justice. We will be training directors to seek out the marginalized and listen for God's prophetic word there. We will be bringing spiritual direction to settings where it has not yet been. We will be moving beyond individualized spirituality toward the deeply spiritual work of community and structural change. We will, in short, become not only friends of God but also prophets.

For Further Reflection

1. What God are we looking for? What God are we helping others to pay attention to?

2. Does your theology embrace the prophetic edge, or shy away from what may be uncomfortable or challenging?

3. Are you globally aware? Do you feel prompted by God's spirit to participate in — or even lead — the vast shifts of consciousness that are shaping our world today: the human rights movement, the environmental movement, etc.? What would this look like in your ministry of spiritual direction?

4. How urgently do you seek out the marginalized to learn from them? Have you experienced this in your formation program? If so, how has this taken place?

Resources

Bonhoeffer, Dietrich. *The Cost of Discipleship.* New York: Macmillan, 1949.

Lonsdale, David. *Handbook of Spirituality for Ministers.* Mahwah, N.J.: Paulist Press, 1995.

Soelle, Dorothee. *The Silent Cry: Mysticism and Resistance.* Minneapolis: Augsburg Fortress Press, 2001.

Notes

1. The Human Experience of God

1. I want to express my gratitude to the five other staff members of the Bread of Life program (Bread of Life Center in Davis, California) who developed and creatively implemented the curriculum based on the Circle of Life: Sandra Lommasson, Joan Stock, Barbara Ernst, Marjorie Hoyer Smith, and Gerry Hair. I also want to acknowledge with gratitude and appreciation many years of creative collaboration on the Mercy Center (Burlingame, California) formation program with Sr. Lorita Moffatt and Janice Farrell. Finally, I want to acknowledge the contribution of my wife, Carmen, who has helped to develop my understanding of the Circle of Life through collaboration on classes and retreats over the past twenty-five years.

3. Hearing with the Heart / Contemplative Listening in the Spiritual Direction Session

2. Throughout this text I will be using the first person plural, because when I teach contemplative listening I do so with a team consisting of another professor and approximately six small-group facilitators. Here, I am especially indebted to Professor Mary Rose Bumpus, with whom I drafted the SFTS curriculum for first-year students.

3. See Simone Weil, "Reflections on the Right Use of School Studies with a View to the Love of God," in *Waiting for God* (New York: G. P. Putnam's Sons, 1951).

4. International Listening Association, 1996, online at *www.listen.org*.

5. Elizabeth Liebert, professor of Christian Spirituality at San Francisco Theological Seminary, originally adapted this practice for use in our program from a book on theological reflection entitled *From Ministry to Theology* (see resources at end of chapter).

5. Waiting on God / Staying with Movements of God

6. From a presentation at Mercy Center, Burlingame, Calif., in February 1990.

7. Walter J. Burghardt, "Contemplation: A Long, Loving Look at the Real," *Church* (Winter 1989).

8. Eliot Rosen and Ellen Burstyn, *Experiencing the Soul: Before Birth, During Life, After Death* (Carlsbad, Calif.: Hay House, 1997).

6. Running from God / Resistance to the Movements of God

9. I am grateful to Marilyn Lacey, RSM, for her generous help in putting into written form in this chapter and in Chapter 5 my experiences from the practice of spiritual direction and the formation of spiritual directors over many years.

10. Jeremiah 20:7.

11. Jeremiah 23:29.

12. Exodus 33:20.

13. Isaiah 55:8.

14. Belden Lane, *The Solace of Fierce Landscapes* (New York: Oxford University Press, 1998), 46.

15. Gerald May, author, mentor of spiritual directors, and dear personal friend who died as this book was being prepared in 2005, wrote that the human mind is "an endless source of inventiveness when it comes to avoiding the implications of spiritual experience," *Care of Mind/Care of Spirit: Psychiatric Dimensions of Spiritual Direction* (San Francisco: HarperSanFrancisco, 1982), 85.

16. Though there is no space here to address it, Ignatius's rules for discernment are especially helpful in sorting out what is taking place in the resisting directee. Cf. *The Spiritual Exercises of St. Ignatius*, trans. Louis J. Puhl (Chicago: Loyola University Press, 1951).

17. I am indebted to Gerald May for delineating many of the forms that resistance can take; see especially chapters five and six of his *Care of Mind/Care of Spirit*. Directors must have a solid grounding in and respect for the psychology of resistance in order to be helpful to the directee. God, after all, works in and through our human experience, not on some parallel "supernatural" track. For an excellent treatment of the psychological dimensions of resistance, see Barry and Connolly's book *The Practice of Spiritual Direction* (San Francisco: HarperSanFrancisco, 1982), chapter 6.

18. Matthew 10:39.

19. Resistance, in the prophetic sense of standing boldly against systemic injustice in the world, can also be the result of conversion wrought by God in our hearts. When it arises in the direction conversation as the darkness of social desolation, the director can assist the directee to recognize God-at-work. For a superb treatment of this contemporary reality, cf. Dorothee Soelle's book *The Silent Cry: Mysticism and Resistance*, trans. Barbara and Martin Rumscheidt (Minneapolis: Fortress Press, 2001).

20. John 15:1–8.

21. Gerald May borrows the phrase "bearing the beams of love" from William Blake for the title of his first chapter in *The Enlightened Heart* (San Francisco: HarperCollins, 1991).

7. Toward Union with God / Development and Transitions in Prayer

22. Teresa of Ávila, *The Interior Castle,* trans. Kieran Kavanaugh and Otilio Rodriguez (Mahwah, N.J.: Paulist Press, 1979).

23. Ibid., 39.

24. Ibid., 57.

25. Ibid., 62.

26. Ibid., 60.

27. Ibid., 65.

28. John's treatment of the three signs can be found in *The Ascent of Mount Carmel,* Book II, chapter 13 and in *The Dark Night of the Soul,* Book I, chapter 9. See *The Collected Works of St. John of the Cross,* trans. Kieran Kavanaugh and Otilio Rodriguez (Washington D.C.: ICS Publications, 1979), 140–41 and 313–16.

29. This interpretation of the second sign is found in Gerald May's book *The Dark Night of the Soul: A Psychiatrist Explores the Connection Between Darkness and Spiritual Growth* (HarperSanFrancisco, 2004), 140.

30. *The Collected Works of St. John of the Cross,* 141.

31. Teresa of Ávila, *The Interior Castle,* 81.

32. Ibid., 179.

33. *The Collected Works of St. John of the Cross,* 608.

34. Teresa of Ávila, *The Collected Works of St. Teresa of Ávila,* vol. 1, trans. Kieran Kavanaugh and Otilio Rodriguez (Washington, D.C.: ICS Publications, 1987), 71.

8. Listening to the Soul's Story / Psychology in Spiritual Direction Programs

35. Heinrich Meng and Ernst L. Freud, eds., *Psychoanalysis and Faith: The Letters of Sigmund Freud and Oskar Pfister* (New York: Basic Books, 1963), 17.

36. Janet Malone, CND, "The Helping Relationships," in *Human Development* 21, no. 4 (Winter, 2000): 5–13.

37. I am indebted to the late Randall Mason of the Center for Religion and Psychotherapy of Chicago and to Emily Haight, former faculty of CRPC for these metaphors.

38. John Veltri, SJ, "For Those Who Accompany Others on Their Inward Journey," in *Orientations,* vol. 2, part B (Guelph, Ont.: Loyola House, 1979), 513–72; see *www.sentex.net/ jveltri/guide/spirit. html*; accessed March 19, 2005.

39. Victor L. Schermer, *Spirit and Psyche: a New Paradigm for Psychology, Psychoanalysis, and Psychotherapy* (London: Jessica Kingsley Publishers, 2003), 27.

40. Nancey Murphy, "Nonreductive Physicalism: Philosophical Issues," in *Whatever Happened to the Soul? Scientific and Theological Portraits of Human Nature,* ed. Warren S. Brown, Nancey Murphy, and H. Newton Maloney, Theology and the Sciences (Minneapolis: Fortress Press, 1998), 147

41. See Ken Wilber, *Integral Psychology: Consciousness, Spirit, Psychology, Therapy* (Boston: Shambhala Publications, 2000) and Ken Wilber, *No Boundary: Eastern and Western Approaches to Personal Growth* (Boston: Shambhala Publications, 1979).

42. Thomas Keating, *Invitation to Love: The Way of Christian Contemplation* (New York: Continuum, 2000), 3.

43. See Schermer, *Psyche and Spirit.* Also Brian Grant, *A Theology for Pastoral Psychotherapy: God's Play in Sacred Spaces* (New York: Haworth Press, 2001) and C. Kevin Gillespie, "Listening for Grace: Self Psychology and Spiritual Direction," in *Handbook of Spirituality for Ministers,* vol. 1, ed. Robert Wicks (Mahwah, N.J.: Paulist Press, 1995), 347–61.

44. Schermer, *Psyche and Spirit,* 70.

45. See W. Harold Grant, Mary Magdala Thompson, and Thomas E. Clarke, *From Image to Likeness: a Jungian Path in the Gospel Journey* (Mahwah, N.J.: Paulist Press, 1983).

46. See James Empereur, *The Enneagram and Spiritual Direction: Nine Paths to Spiritual Guidance* (New York: Continuum, 1997).

47. For Erikson see Erik Erikson, *Childhood and Society* (New York: W. W. Norton & Company, 1950) and Evelyn Eaton Whitehead and James D. Whitehead, *Christian Life Patterns: the Psychological Challenges and Religious Invitations of Adult Life,* new ed. (New York: Crossroad, 1992). For Kegan see Robert Kegan, *The Evolving Self: Problems and Process in Human Development* (Cambridge: Harvard University Press, 1982) and Elizabeth Liebert, *Changing Life Patterns: Adult Development in Spiritual Direction,* 2nd ed. (Atlanta: Chalice Press, 2001). For both see Walter E. Conn, *The Desiring Self: Rooting Pastoral Counseling and Spiritual Direction in Self-Transcendence* (Mahwah, N.J.: Paulist Press, 1998).

48. Liebert, *Changing Life Patterns,* 74.

49. Gerald May, *Care of Mind/Care of Spirit: Psychiatric Dimensions of Spiritual Direction* (San Francisco: HarperSanFrancisco, 1982), 123–47.

50. See William A. Barry and William J. Connolly, *The Practice of Spiritual Direction* (San Francisco: HarperSanFrancisco, 1982), 155–74.

51. Gerard Egan, *The Skilled Helper: A Problem-Management and Opportunity-Development Approach to Helping* (Stamford, Conn.: Wadsworth Publishing, 2004).

52. See Kelly Bulkeley, *The Wilderness of Dreams: Exploring the Religious Meaning of Dreams in Modern Western Culture* (Albany: State University of New York Press, 1994). Also Robert Johnson, *Inner Work: Using Dreams and Active Imagination for Personal Growth* (San Francisco: HarperSanFrancisco, 1986) and Jeremy Taylor, *Where People Fly and Water Runs Uphill: Using Dreams to Tap the Power of the Unconscious* (New York: Warner Books, 1992).

53. Barry and Connolly, *The Practice of Spiritual Direction,* 179.

9. Maturing in Faith / Stages in the Adult Spiritual Journey

54. Richard Byrne, "Journey (Growth and Development in Spiritual Life)," *The New Dictionary Of Catholic Spirituality* (Collegeville, Minn.: Liturgical Press, 1993), 571–72. The particular names for the stages described by John of the Cross are from a presentation by Paul V. Robb, "On Becoming a Spiritual Companion," given at Campion Renewal Center in Weston, Mass. on March 19, 1991.

55. James W. Fowler, *Stages Of Faith: The Psychology Of Human Development and the Quest For Meaning* (San Francisco: HarperSanFrancisco, 1981). Fowler offers six stages for the total cycle. This article draws on the latter four.

56. Murray Stein, *Jung's Map of the Soul* (Chicago: Open Court, 1998) offers an excellent secondary resource for Jung's individuation process.

57. Fowler, *Stages of Faith,* 151–73.

58. Stein, *Jung's Map,* 108–20.

59. Fowler, *Stages of Faith,* 174–83.

60. Stein, *Jung's Map,* 13–30.

61. Fowler, *Stages of Faith,* 184–98.

62. John A. Sanford, *Evil: The Shadow Side of Reality* (New York: Crossroad, 1981), 49–66.

63. James W. Fowler, *Faithful Change* (Nashville: Abingdon Press, 1996), 89–144, and James M. Bowler, SJ, "Shame: A Primary Root of Resistance to Movement in Direction," *Presence* (September 1997): 25–33.

64. Fowler, *Stages of Faith,* 199–211.

65. Stein, *Jung's Map,* 151–69.

66. John Macmurray, *The Self as Agent,* 3rd ed. (London: Humanities Press International, 1991), 217–22.

67. Janet K. Ruffing, *Spiritual Direction: Beyond the Beginnings* (Mahwah, N.J.: Paulist Press, 2000), 125–54.

68. William A. Barry and William J. Connolly, *The Practice of Spiritual Direction* (San Francisco: HarperSanFrancisco, 1982), 8.

10. Embracing the Wisdom of the Body / Feelings and Spiritual Direction

69. The Enneagram system is detailed in many books. A good place to begin is Suzanne Zuercher, OSB, *Enneagram Spirituality* (Notre Dame, Ind.: Ave Maria Press, 1992). A more complete bibliography is provided at the end of this paper.

70. Eugene Gendlin first described the focusing process. His book *Focusing* (New York: Bantam Books, 1981) is still an excellent source of information about this process. A more complete bibliography for focusing information is contained at the end of this paper.

11. Tending the Sacred Fire / Sexuality and Spiritual Direction

71. See Donald Evans, *Spirituality and Human Nature* (Albany, N.Y.: SUNY Press, 1992).

72. Ronald Rolheiser, *The Holy Longing: The Search for a Christian Spirituality* (New York: Doubleday, 1999), 202.

73. Ibid., 193.

74. Diarmuid O'Murchu, *Quantum Theology* (New York: Crossroad, 1997), 21.

75. *Keter Shem Tov* 41, no. 16.

76. *Jerusalem Talmud*, Kiddushin 4:12.

77. *Confessions*, 10.27.

78. Yancey, "Sex, Lies, and Life on the Evangelical Edge" (available at *www.sojo.net*).

79. Rolheiser, *The Holy Longing*, 193.

80. Brian Swimme, *The Universe Is a Green Dragon* (Santa Fe, N.Mex.: Bear and Company, 1985), 43–52.

81. Rolheiser, *The Holy Longing*, 194, 196, 198.

82. McMahon and Campbell, *A Biospiritual Approach to Sexuality: Healing a Spirituality of Control* (Kansas City, Mo.: Sheed and Ward, 1991), 4.

83. Ferder and Heagle, *Your Sexual Self: Pathway to Authentic Intimacy* (Notre Dame, Ind.: Ave Maria Press, 1992), 43–44.

84. Ibid., 24.

85. Ibid., 32–33.

86. See Michael Washburn, *Transpersonal Psychology in Psychoanalytic Perspective* (New York: SUNY Press, 1999).

87. Rolheiser, *The Holy Longing*, 199.

88. Matthew Fox, *Illuminations of Hildegard of Bingen* (Santa Fe, N.Mex.: Bear and Company, 1985), 30–33, 63–65.

13. Surviving (and Thriving) as Supervisors / Some Dynamics of a Supervisory Program

89. Baird K. Brightman, PhD, "Narcissistic Issues in the Training Experience of the Psychotherapist," *International Journal of Psychoanalytic Psychotherapy* 12 (1983). Narcissism is discussed as a dynamic element in the struggle for psychic growth, involving "a positive libidinal feeling toward the self" or the maintenance of self-esteem in the face of the erosion of one's grandiose professional self and of one's projection of perfection onto others, namely, the staff, the supervisor. Brightman sees a clinical program "as a developmental period of adulthood with its own characteristic tasks and demands, and therefore the potential for evoking the conflicts, fixations, and defenses of the preceding life stages (as well as the potential for further growth)."

14. Spiritual Direction in Community / Layers of Relationship

90. Miriam Greenspan, "Out of Bounds," *Common Boundary* (July–August 1995): 56.

91. Katherine Hancock Ragsdale, ed., *Boundary Wars: Intimacy and Distance in Healing Relationships* (Cleveland: Pilgrim Press, 1996), xix.

92. "Guidelines for Ethical Conduct," Spiritual Directors International, 3.

93. The lifeframe or grid is used in many formation programs as an awareness tool. It has four major arenas of life: the intrapersonal or interior, the interpersonal or more informal realm of relationship, the structural realm of role and formal relationship, and the environmental arena or larger field within which movements of history, culture, nature, and anthropology hold and influence all others arenas. See James, Keegan, SJ, "To Bring All Things Together" *Presence* 1, no. 1 (1995).

94. Sandra Lommasson Pickens, "Looking at Dual/Multiple Relationships," *Presence* 2, no. 2 (1996): 54–55.

95. Douglas Steere, *Gleanings: A Random Harvest* (Nashville: Upper Room, 1997).

96. Thomas Hedberg and Betsy Caprio, *A Code of Ethics for Spiritual Directors* (Pecos, N.Mex.: Dove Publications, 1992).

97. Ibid., 8.

98. Ragsdale, *Boundary Wars,* xxi.

99. Lommasson Pickens, "Looking at Dual/Multiple Relationships," 56.

100. Karen Lebacqz and Joseph D. Driskill, *Ethics and Spiritual Care* (Nashville: Abingdon Press, 2000), 70–71.

101. Ibid., 71, 76.

102. Lommasson Pickens, "Looking at Dual/Multiple Relationships," 57.

103. Ragsdale, *Boundary Wars,* 79.

16. Widening the Tent / Spiritual Practice Across Traditions

104. Karen Armstrong, Karen, *The Battle for God* (New York: Ballantine Publishing Group, 2000), xiv–xv.

105. I write this from my own experience on the Coordinating Council of Spiritual Directors International in which we began to interview staff from a variety of formation programs in the United States for information about changes in the ministry. Reflections from other countries and cultures are needed to round out this necessarily parochial perspective.

106. Diarmuid O'Murchu, *Reclaiming Spirituality* (New York: Crossroad, 1998), 12.

107. Don Bisson, FMS, presentation July 11–16, 2003, on "A Jungian-Christian Dialogue: Toward the Healing of Christianity."

108. George Barna, Barna Research Group, press release February 25, 1999.

109. Pat Luce and Bob Schmitt, "Looking Beyond Our Tradition: an Invitation to Christian Spiritual Directors," *Presence: An International Journal of Spiritual Direction* 2, no. 3 (1996): 12.

110. Robert C. Fuller, "Spiritual, but Not Religious," *www.beliefnet.com/story/109/story_10958_1.html.*

111. Owen C. Thomas, "Political Spirituality: Oxymoron or Redundancy?" *Journal of Religion and Society. http://moses.creighton.edu/JRS/2001/2001-3.html.*

112. Thomas Hart, *Spiritual Quest: A Guide to the Changing Landscape* (Mahwah, N.J.: Paulist Press, 1999), 40.

113. Ronald Rolheiser, *The Holy Longing: The Search for a Christian Spirituality* (New York: Doubleday, 1999), concepts from chapter 1, "What Is Spirituality?"

114. Hart, *Spiritual Quest,* 43.

115. Robert Wuthnow, *After Heaven: Spirituality in America since the 1950s* (Berkeley and Los Angeles: University of California Press, 1998o, chapter 7.

116. Howard Addison, *Show Me Your Way: The Complete Guide to Exploring Interfaith Spiritual Direction* (Woodstock, Vt.: Skylight Paths Publishing, 2000), 172.

117. Dalai Lama, *The Good Heart: A Buddhist Perspective on the Teachings of Jesus* (Boston: Wisdom Publications, 1996), 79.

118. Wuthnow, *After Heaven,* 17.

119. Hart, *Spiritual Quest,* 49.

120. Griffiths, *The New Creation in Christ,* 96–97.

121. Don Bisson, "Jungian-Christian Dialogue: The Jesus Wound," Davis-Auburn retreat, July 2003.

122. Addison, *Show Me Your Way,* xi–xii.

123. Ibid., 146–47.

124. M. Robert Mulholland, "Life at the Center — Life at the Edge." *Weavings* (July–August 1998).

18. Cultivating a New Generation / Formation of Future Spiritual Directors

125. Kristen Wensing, "A National Conversation on Generational Ethics," Duke University on June 24, 2002, *www.contentofourcharacter.org*.

126. Nantais, "Whatever Is Not Ignatian Indifference," 5.

127. Tom Beaudoin, *Virtual Faith: The Irreverent Spiritual Quest of Generation X* (San Francisco: Jossey-Bass, 1998), 2.

128. David Nantais, "Whatever Is Not Ignatian Indifference," 5.

20. Friends of God and Prophets / Transformation for Justice

129. Dorothee Soelle, *The Silent Cry: Mysticism and Resistance,* trans. Barbara and Martin Rumscheidt (Minneapolis: Fortress Press, 2001).

130. Ibid.

131. Abraham Joshua Heschel, *The Prophets* (New York: HarperCollins, 2001), 16, 231.

132. Grace Jantzen, *Power, Gender and Christian Mysticism* (Cambridge: Cambridge University Press, 1995), 329.

133. Walter J. Burghardt, "Contemplation: A Long, Loving Look at the Real," *Church* (Winter 1989).

Author Biographies

Bro. Donald Bisson, FMS, DMin, holds an MA in Christian Spirituality from Creighton University, an MA in Liturgy from Notre Dame, an MA in Transpersonal Studies from the Institute of Transpersonal Psychology, and a DMin from the Pacific School of Religion. Don is a former Mercy Center staff member and is currently on the leadership team of the Marist Brothers. Don is a formator of spiritual directors, a workshop presenter, and consultant. He specializes in Jungian psychology.

Maria Tattu Bowen, PhD, has extensive experience teaching, lecturing, writing, and ministering in both Roman Catholic and Protestant settings, including the Graduate Theological Union in Berkeley, California, and the Doctoral Program in Spiritual Direction at San Francisco Theological Seminary. She has worked as a spiritual director since 1985 and has supervised spiritual directors since 1996. Her practice includes laypeople, seminary students, clergy, and religious women and men. For more information, please visit her Web site at *www.mariatattubowen.com.*

James M. Bowler, SJ, is Facilitator for Catholic and Jesuit Mission and Identity at Fairfield University in Fairfield, Connecticut. He formerly served on the staff at Loyola House in Guelph, Ontario, Canada. For more than fifteen years he has incorporated a psychospiritual approach to Ignatian spirituality in his ministry of direction, supervision, and training. The work from which this article grew was made possible through participation in programs at the C. G. Jung Institutes in Zurich and Boston as well as through a fellowship at the Center for Research in Faith and Moral Development at the Candler School of Theology of Emory University.

Suzanne M. Buckley, General Editor, is Manager of Mission Advancement at Mercy Center, Burlingame, California, where she completed her spiritual direction formation in 1992. In her corporate life (1980s) she developed training programs for Fortune 500 companies. An educator, spiritual director, and supervisor of spiritual directors, she is an adjunct professor at the University of San Francisco as well as program staff for the Summer Internship in Spiritual Direction at Mercy Center. Suzanne holds a BS in Organizational Development and an MA in Applied Spirituality.

Patricia Coughlin, OSB, is a member of the Benedictine Sisters of Chicago. She has been a teacher of writing and literature at the secondary level as well as a trainer of intern spiritual directors at the Institute for Spiritual Leadership in Chicago. Currently she is in private practice as a pastoral psychotherapist in Chicago. She is a graduate of the spiritual directors training program at the Institute for Spiritual Leadership and of the Center for Religion and Psychotherapy of Chicago. She holds a DMin from the Chicago Theological Seminary. For many years she has been giving retreats and workshops on dreams and spirituality around the world.

Bill Creed, SJ, is a Jesuit priest in Chicago who has been involved in spiritual direction and the forming of spiritual directors for thirty years. With Michael Sparough, SJ, Mary Guido, RC, and Mary Sharon Riley, RC, he currently co-leads an initial seven-month internship in spiritual direction and with Julie Murray a summer advanced internship in the Spiritual Exercises of St. Ignatius Loyola.

Rose Mary Dougherty, SSND, is Senior Fellow for Spiritual Guidance for Shalem Institute for Spiritual Formation in Bethesda, Maryland. She currently serves as a volunteer at Joseph's House, an AIDS hospice for homeless men, and offers retreats and spiritual direction primarily for hospice caregivers.

Joseph D. Driskill, PhD, is Associate Professor of Spirituality and Dean of the Disciples Seminary Foundation, Berkeley, California. He does spiritual direction as a staff member of the Lloyd Center, San Francisco Theological Seminary. Driskill holds ministerial standing with the Christian Church (Disciples of Christ) in the USA and Canada and the United Church of Canada. He has been the pastor of churches in Missouri, Kentucky, and Saskatchewan, and served for twelve years in London, Ontario, as a campus minister. His publications include *Protestant Spiritual Exercises: Theology, History, and Practice* (Morehouse, 1999); *Ethics and Spiritual Care,* coauthored with Karen Lebacqz (Abingdon, 2000); chapters in *Religious and Social Ritual: Interdisciplinary Explorations* (SUNY, 1996) and *Still Listening: New Horizons in Spiritual Direction* (Morehouse, 2000); and articles in *Presence, Pastoral Psychology,* and the *American Journal of Pastoral Counseling.*

Janice B. Farrell, MA, a Mercy Center adjunct staff member since 1992, holds an MA in psychology, state certification in holistic health education and counseling, and postgraduate studies in theology from the Jesuit School of Theology, Berkeley. Through Kairos Support for Caregivers in San Francisco, Janice has done extensive work with caregivers of those with chronic and terminal illnesses. Janice was also the founder and director of the Source Center for Spiritual Development and Wholeness in San Francisco. Her primary ministry is spiritual direction, group spiritual direction, retreat direction, and the formation of spiritual directors. Janice has a special interest in humanistic and transpersonal psychologies, the spirituality of the arts, the earth, and all faith traditions.

James M. Keegan, SJ, is a Jesuit priest of the New England Province. His major interests are doing spiritual direction and directed retreats, and training and supervising directors. Jim is a graduate of the Center for Religious Development in Cambridge, Massachusetts, and was the first graduate to work full time on that staff — from 1985 to 1989. For four years before that he was a team member and director of Campion Renewal Center in Weston, Massachusetts. In Louisville, Kentucky, from 1990 to 2001, he was part of the team of the Archdiocesan Office of Ministry and Spirituality. There he worked with priests and laypeople, did lots of spiritual direction, and ran six two-year practicum programs for the development of spiritual directors. In 2002 he returned to New England where he serves as director of Eastern Point Retreat House. Jim is also a member of the Coordinating Council of Spiritual Directors International and was part of the editorial board that founded the journal *Presence.*

Sandra Lommasson is the founder and executive director of the Bread of Life Center for Spiritual Formation based in Davis, California. She received her formation as a spiritual director at Mercy Center in Burlingame, California. Currently, Sandra's primary ministry is in the development and supervision of spiritual directors as well as the formation of leaders tending the Spirit within churches or public organizations. She is also very involved in new program development and is a published author in the field of spiritual formation. In addition to her work at Bread of Life, Sandra has served on the Council of Spiritual Directors International since 1999 and as its president since 2001. She is mother to two grown children and delights in one very special grandson.

James Neafsey, DMin, has been a spiritual director, retreat leader, and teacher of Christian spirituality since 1974. He has taught spirituality classes at John F. Kennedy University, the California Institute of Integral Studies, Santa Clara University, and the School of Applied Theology in Oakland. For the past ten years he has taught and supervised in ecumenical formation programs for spiritual directors at Mercy Center, Burlingame, California, and the Bread of Life Center, Davis, California. He holds an MDiv from Weston School of Theology and a DMin in Art and Spirituality from the Graduate Theological Foundation. Jim's other professional interests include transpersonal psychology and comparative mysticism.

Mary Ann Scofield, RSM, PhD, a staff member of Mercy Center, Burlingame, California, holds a PhD in Theology, an MA in Spiritual Direction, and is a founding member of Spiritual Directors International. Mary Ann's ministry is primarily the formation of spiritual directors and supervisors, spiritual and retreat direction, and supervision of spiritual directors. She has also done work in the formation of directors in Thailand, Kenya, Lithuania, Ireland, Alaska, and Hawaii.

Lucy Abbott Tucker prepared for the ministry of spiritual direction at the Institute for Spiritual Leadership in Chicago. She has been teaching on the staff there since 1988. Lucy teaches a class titled Personal Transformation for Mission and is involved in spiritual direction, supervision, focusing, and Enneagram work. She chaired the committee that prepared the "Guidelines for Ethical Conduct" of Spiritual Directors International. Lucy has been involved in training programs throughout the United States, Canada, and Europe. She is a married laywoman and lives in Chicago with her husband, Thomas.

Acknowledgments

This book is the cooperative effort of spiritual directors engaged in the ministry of formation from a variety of programs throughout the United States. Without their generosity of time, talent, and spirit, *Sacred Is the Call* would not have been possible. I am grateful to the authors and the programs that they represent:

Mercy Center, Burlingame, California
Bread of Life Center, Davis, California
Shalem Institute for Spiritual Formation, Bethesda, Maryland
San Francisco Theological Seminary and the Diploma in the Art
    of Spiritual Direction, San Anselmo, California
the Institute for Spiritual Leadership in Chicago
the Internship in Spiritual Direction at Loyola University, Chicago
the Center for Religious Development, Cambridge, Massachusetts
the Linwood Spiritual Center in Rhinebeck, New York

The text reflects the guidance and wisdom of Mary Ann Scofield, RSM. Her experience in the formation of spiritual directors, her deep knowledge of the ministry and her wide field of respected colleagues helped move this text from idea to reality. I am also indebted to Jim Keegan, SJ, for his ongoing advice and humor throughout the project. The support of the religious leadership team at Mercy Burlingame, and in particular the loving endorsement of Sr. Mary Waskowiak for this endeavor, has been invaluable.

Those on the Mercy Center formation staff who are not represented in the text — Sr. Lorita Moffatt, Sr. Mary Ann Clifford, Catherine Regan — need to be recognized for their ongoing contributions to the ministry and thanked for their encouragement as this project came to fruition. I appreciate Diarmuid Rooney, Director of Mercy Center, for understanding the value of going forward with this publication despite many competing demands on my time.

This project was made more manageable by the able technical support I received from Mark Werlin, and the skill of our wonderful copy editor, Jean Blomquist.

I remember with much gratitude my experience of transformative learning during the Summer Internship in the Art of Spiritual Direction at Mercy Center.

I am thankful to my colleagues on that staff who have not yet been mentioned — especially Marguerite Buchanan, RSM; Joe McHugh, SJ; Kathleen Geelan; Bob Thesing, SJ; Miriam Cleary, OSU; Jean Evans, RSM; Sr. Jean Sauntry; Garry Schmidtt; and Fr. Rick Fredrichs; whose gifts have helped many interns to discern the call to spiritual direction.

My husband, Ken Dunckel, and our son, Patrick Buckley-Dunckel, have provided me with love and stability as I have journeyed into this ministry over the past sixteen years. I could not do this work without them.

And finally, Roy M. Carlisle, senior editor at the Crossroad Publishing Company, believed in this project and its neophyte editor. Roy shepherded this book with grace and élan, and I am most grateful for his support and kindness.

SUZANNE M. BUCKLEY

A Word from the Publisher

I walked into a community church in Berkeley that weekend mostly out of curiosity. I was attending a regional meeting of Spiritual Directors International, and I wanted to know more about this organization I had just joined and learn more about others in the field who would attend. The SDI journal *Presence* was becoming more and more important to me as encouragement in my own spiritual journey. It was enhancing the work I had done in my own spiritual direction, which had been formative for me. So now I was also wondering about finding new authors and writers for books in this field. The lecture was interesting, but providentially I met Suzanne Buckley that afternoon. She was the regional coordinator for SDI, and she also worked at Mercy Center in Burlingame, one of the best-known spiritual direction training program centers in the country. Suzanne is one of those women who move through the world with purpose and confidence. And she is warm and delightful to engage. She approached me with an idea for a book, and what she told me piqued my interest immediately.

Although most editors don't really talk about what I call the "completion factor," it is an essential intuitive act of judgment in the work of an acquisition and development editor like myself. In other words I have to make a decision, usually with very little data, on whether the person or writer I am conversing with can actually complete a project. My intuition goes into overdrive on this factor because as publishers we really can't afford to contract for a book with an author and not have that project completed and delivered. At least not very often. Don't get me wrong. I have made this mistake more than once in my career, and even recently, but you could count my failures in this regard on the fingers of one hand because I know how critical it is for our business to be extremely careful in this regard. But it is a failure almost like no other for a senior editor, and it hits me hard when I put all of my years of experience and skill and effort into making a project happen and it doesn't. My initial instinct was that if Suzanne was going to try to put together a book on spiritual direction with the help of other spiritual directors in this field, she had the moxie to make it happen. The truth is that I do trust my intuitional instincts, and in this instance I was making an accurate assessment.

But writing a book or, in Suzanne's case, compiling and editing a book, is a monumental task. There are no shortcuts, there are no easy ways to do it, and it will tax the abilities of everyone involved, no matter who they are, even writers who have done it before. So I have to make this judgment in each case for each book almost as if nothing had been done in the past. Obviously if someone has done it previously, it does give me some indication that that person might be able to do it again. But every book is its own revelation of that writer's or editor's soul in a new way each time, and with each new project the energy and effort required doesn't diminish because he or she has done it before. There are a thousand reasons why this time it won't be completed. It is one of those tasks that very few people can actually accomplish, although practically everyone I meet says they would like to do it. Why is it that everyone wants to write a book? And why do scores of people who have no training in writing think they can, especially the act of long distance writing, as I like to think about what it means to write a book? (I am a runner so this image works for me.) That has always been a mystery to me. And Suzanne had never done this before. But she had managed large projects for her work in the corporate world before she became a part of the staff at Mercy Center. That was encouraging to hear. So I was all ears when she began to formulate her vision for this venture.

In August of 2004 I went to Mercy Center to meet with Suzanne and also to meet Diarmuid Rooney, the director of the Center, and Sr. Mary Ann Scofield, the founder of the training programs and an internationally recognized leader in the formation and training of

spiritual directors. Out of our conversations that afternoon and subsequent ones over the weeks emerged a strategy for doing a series
of books, the first of which you hold in your hands. It was an am-
bitious vision and strategy, but the more I got to know Suzanne the
more I realized that this woman doesn't have the word "can't" in her
vocabulary. So we began.

There were the usual ups and downs of trying to coordinate a whole
host of contributors and make sure what they wrote would really "fit"
the scheme for the book. But the biggest setback was when Suzanne
herself fell ill with pneumonia. (I know we do live in California, but
it happens.) Suzanne was not to be denied, and she continued to
coordinate efforts from her sickbed and make it seem like it was
normal to manage a project of this magnitude even in her diminished
physical capacity. She prevailed, of course, and we hardly missed a
beat. Frankly, I think it was a stunning accomplishment.

It was my distinct pleasure and privilege to get to know Suzanne,
Sr. Mary Ann, Sandra Lommasson, and other contributors to this
volume over the course of months that we worked on the book. In
each case I was reminded of how dedicated this group of trainers
and spiritual directors really are. They all volunteered vast amounts
of time and energy not just because they felt called to do so but also
so that the proceeds generated from the sales of the book could be
used to fund programs at the Center.

The growing ministry of spiritual direction is cutting across all
sectarian lines and even across faith barriers. It is a ministry that
is helping individuals discover the presence of God in their own
faith journey and so revitalize an experience of personal transformation that has been long neglected in many branches of the Christian
church and in streams of faith that flow from other religious traditions. And it is a ministry that is quite distinct from pastoral
counseling, psychotherapy, or preaching and teaching. I know that I
speak for all of us involved in this project when I say that we hope
this volume will contribute needed information and guidance in the
training of spiritual directors, encourage the setting up of new training programs, and provide a core curriculum for trainees and trainers

to use in their own work of ministry. A book is only one tool in a range of resources needed to build faith and community, but we are proud to contribute this new tool to the field.

As an editor and publisher I am always grateful to writers and authors for the act of courage and generosity that produces a book. In this case, though, I want to extend my personal thanks and a professional thank you on behalf of The Crossroad Publishing Company to everyone who contributed to this volume and especially to Suzanne Buckley and Sr. Mary Ann Scofield, whose tireless efforts really did make this happen.